The Tower Air Fryer Cookbook 2023

550 Days Affordable, Effortless and Mouthwatering Tower Air Fryer Recipes for Beginners to have Fun Cooking and Eating

Sarah Collins

Table of Contents

Chapter 8 Beef, Pork, and Lamb   44

Chapter 9 Desserts   53

INTRODUCTION

When it comes to kitchen and other home appliances, Tower is one of the world's largest manufacturers, serving markets worldwide. Having been around for over a century, theirs is one of the most recognizable brands on the market.

It's therefore unsurprising that Tower is also a leading brand in the air fryer market. With over ten different air fryer models, one can easily argue that they have an air fryer for everybody, irrespective of budget and family size.

Choosing the Tower air fryer was an easy decision for me. Given the pedigree they've garnered over the years and my experience using some of their other products, I just knew it had to be Tower when it came time for me to purchase an air fryer. And, so far, I have not been disappointed.

Since you're here, I can safely assume that you've just recently purchased your Tower air fryer and are looking for ways to get the best out of your new equipment. You've come to the right place.

This cookbook will give you a basic overview of your air fryer and how it works to help you become familiar with the appliance and make your navigation easy. Much more than that, though, I'll hold your hands and lead you on an adventure into the world of recipes your air fryer makes possible.

Depending on how vast you are in this recipe world, we may move from the very familiar to the exotic but strange. And I can assure you that you'll not only venture into new cooking horizons but also discover novel ways to get better results at what you've done practically your whole life.

This cookbook is not some distant, dispassionate rendering of instructions that many are wont to. Rather, I'll be sharing my experience as a fellow sojourner who has gone ahead of you on this journey, pushed by the same desires that now propel you, the desire to bring life and vitality into our kitchen and to conquer new worlds from its walls.

There's not one of the recipes you'll come across in this book that I've not made myself. And that's why the instructions are clear and direct, often coming with tips I've garnered from years of making them. I have also carefully chosen the recipes to ensure that the ingredients are easily accessible.

It promises to be quite an adventure. Shall we get started?

Chapter 1 Tower Air Fryer Basic Guide

Chapter 1 Tower Air Fryer Basic Guide

Without a doubt, Tower is a household name regarding kitchen appliances and other housewares. Thankfully, their air fryers have followed the same pattern, continuing a long line of quality and reliability. With a range of air fryers 20 products strong, Tower air fryers are one of the most popular brands you can find in the market today.

Tower air fryers stand out for one unique feature: the vortex air frying technology. And their varying features, capacities, and prices endear them to a broader section of the market, increasing their popularity.

How Does the Tower Air Fryer Work?

The Tower air fryer is an electricity-powered appliance that uses vortex air frying technology to fry foods placed in it.

Frying typically involves cooking by dipping food in fats or oils that we then heat until the food is done. With its air frying technology, the Tower air fryer reduces oil and fat usage to the barest minimum and still achieves even better frying results than traditional frying.

The Tower air fryer consists of two major parts: the fryer's body and drawer. The fryer body contains a heating mechanism that heats the air, while the drawer contains a basket that holds your food while it's frying. The basket comes with vents on all sides to allow for hot air circulation around the food for even frying. Apart from providing room for your food while in the air fryer, the drawer also collects excess liquid from your food.

This is what happens when your air fryer is working: a heating element within the air fryer generates heat. A fan speedily circulates the air around the food for even quick cooking, saving you time and giving your food that crispy feel you've always desired.

5 Basic Features of Tower Air Fryers

The following features make Tower air fryers a leading brand in the market:

Less Fat

Tower air fryers help give your food the same crispy feel that deep fryers give while using very little oil or fats. Frying with this appliance significantly reduces the amount of oil in your food and the fat you consume. Ultimately, this appliance gives you the best of both worlds: the crispy feel from fried foods and reduced calorie intake.

Faster Meals

Imagine cooking 500g of fries in 20 minutes! Lightning speed, right? That's what Tower air fryers offer you. With these air fryers, you can reduce your cooking time significantly, allowing you more time for other meaningful engagements. And the next time you're tempted to place an order for that fast food just for its speed, you'd remember you can make something healthier in the same time frame.

More Meal Choices

One of the best features of the Tower air fryers is their versatility. Be it easy appetizers, mains and veggies, or desserts, these appliances can help you produce tantalizing meals within minutes. You may soon find out that you no longer need your oven. And if you've ever dreamt of regularly surprising your family with new recipes, now is the time to live that dream.

Less Energy

With Tower air fryers, you can save up to 50% on your energy bills compared to an oven. This saving is possible because of the speed at which it cooks, which means it doesn't use as much power as your oven would. This feature can be a great benefit in these days of soaring energy prices.

Enough Capacity

While Tower air fryers come in different capacities, they are typically big enough to make a meal for a family of four at once. And if you're living alone and want something for personal meals, there's a tower air fryer for you too.

Select Your Tower Air Fryer

One of the things I love about the Tower air fryers is how they seem to have a product for everyone. No matter the size of your family, budget, or taste, I'm sure you can get an air fryer that suits you from Tower's range of air fryers. Now, let's do a brief rundown of these products according to the variables I've identified.

If yours is a large family and you want an air fryer with maximum capacity, I doubt you can get a better deal than the Tower Vortx XL 14.5L 5-in-1 Digital Air Fryer Oven with Rotisserie Black. This air fryer is big enough to cook a complete meal for your family. Apart from its extra-large capacity, which is 85% larger than the standard air fryer size, it also comes with 16 preset menus and a three-year warranty.

And if you want something big enough but not too big, you have several 12 and 11-litre Tower air fryers to choose from. There are the Vortx 12 Litre Air Fryer Oven Grey and Rose Gold with ten preset options and the Vortx 12 Litre Air Fryer Oven.

On the other end of the size spectrum are several other options, including the super small Vortx 2 Litre Air Fryer, the Vortx 3.2 Litre Manual Air Fryer Black, which is perfect for cooking one or two-portion meals, and the more averagely-sized Vortx 4.3 Litre Family Digital Air Fryer.

There are also many medium-sized options between the extra-large and small-capacity products, including the Vortx 9 Litre Dual Basket Air Fryer and the Vortx Vision 7 Litre Digital Air Fryer and its manual equivalent.

The Vortex 3.2L manual air fryer is generally considered the best budget air fryer among the lot. It comes with vortex air frying technology and four cooking functions, including air frying, grilling, roasting, and baking. And at just about £60, it offers great value for money and enough capacity for a growing family.

We can make a broader distinction among the products in the Tower air fryer range in their operational mode. If you prefer digital appliances, up to seven options across different capacities may appeal to you. Although expectedly pricier than their manual counterparts, some of these digital options are also quite reasonably priced.

Whatever your financial circumstances or functionality that's most important to you, there's most likely a Tower air fryer for you. And whichever one you finally decide upon, you can rest assured that you'd be getting all of the benefits of using the vortex air frying technology that has made the Tower air fryer such a huge success.

Tower Air Fryer Cooking Tips

The following tips can help you get the best results out of your Tower air fryer and make the most amazing recipes:

Before First Use

The first step is to unbox your new appliance and remove all stickers and labels. Then you want to check to ensure that there are no visible damages to the cord or any other body part. You may want to return the air fryer if there are any damages. If you find no damage to the appliance, you can go ahead to clean the basket and drawer with warm water, dishwashing liquid, and a non-abrasive sponge. With a moist tower, wipe the interior and exterior of the appliance clean. Then find a stable, horizontal, and heat-resistant surface to place the air fryer.

Using Your Appliance

To use your Tower air fryer, ensure that there are no items on or around the air fryer, especially close to the vent. Then plug it into an electricity source. Open the drawer and fill the basket with your food. Please note that you do NOT need to fill the drawer with oil or any other liquid. Return the drawer and the basket into the air fryer, and, using the manual as a guide, determine the preparation time and required temperature for the meal and set the timer and temperature control dials appropriately. If you're using the appliance in a cold state, add three minutes to the time. Setting the timer and temperature should turn on your appliance.

While Cooking

For many recipes, you may need to shake the food while cooking. You can do this simply by pulling the drawer by the handle out of the appliance and shaking it. Take extra care not to press the basket release button on the handle while shaking the drawer. Once you're done, return the drawer to the air fryer and continue cooking. The timer bell will ring when the set cooking time elapses. When it does, open the drawer to check if the food is completely cooked. If not, you can cook for a few extra minutes.

How to Care for and Clean Your Tower Air Fryer

Having expended that much money on acquiring your Tower air fryer, you must take all necessary care to ensure that you get appropriate value for your money for the longest possible time. Cleaning your appliance regularly, typically after every use, is one of the surest ways to ensure the air fryer continues to serve you well.

Ensure that the air fryer is unplugged and completely cool before you commence cleaning. Removing the drawer can help you hasten the cooling process. Of the two major parts of the appliance, only the drawer and the baskets require thorough washing with soapy water and a non-abrasive sponge. Take care not to use abrasive cleaning materials on these items as they might lose the non-stick coating.

Wiping the outer body with a moist towel will suffice for the main air fryer body. Use hot water, a non-abrasive sponge to clean the interior, and a cleaning brush to remove residues on the heating element.

When dirt gets stuck to the basket or the bottom of the drawer, fill the drawer with hot water and some washing-up liquid. Then put the basket in the drawer and let them soak for up to 10 minutes.

Chapter 2 Breakfasts

Chapter 2 Breakfasts

Breakfast Sausage and Cauliflower

Prep time: 5 minutes | Cook time: 45 minutes | Serves 4

450 g sausage meat, cooked and crumbled
475 ml double/whipping cream
1 head cauliflower, chopped
235 ml grated Cheddar cheese,
plus more for topping
8 eggs, beaten
Salt and ground black pepper, to taste

Preheat the air fryer to 176°C.

In a large bowl, mix the sausage, cream, chopped cauliflower, cheese and eggs. Sprinkle with salt and ground black pepper.

Pour the mixture into a greased casserole dish. Bake in the preheated air fryer for 45 minutes or until firm.

Top with more Cheddar cheese and serve.

Banana-Nut Muffins

Prep time: 5 minutes | Cook time: 15 minutes | Makes 10 muffins

Oil, for spraying
2 very ripe bananas
120 ml packed light brown sugar
80 ml rapeseed oil or vegetable oil
1 large egg
1 teaspoon vanilla extract
180 ml plain flour
1 teaspoon baking powder
1 teaspoon ground cinnamon
120 ml chopped walnuts

Preheat the air fryer to 160°C. Spray 10 silicone muffin cups lightly with oil.

In a medium bowl, mash the bananas. Add the brown sugar, rapeseed oil, egg, and vanilla and stir to combine.

Fold in the flour, baking powder, and cinnamon until just combined. Add the walnuts and fold a few times to distribute throughout the batter.

Divide the batter equally among the prepared muffin cups and place them in the basket. You may need to work in batches, depending on the size of your air fryer.

Cook for 15 minutes, or until golden brown and a toothpick inserted into the center of a muffin comes out clean. The air fryer tends to brown muffins more than the oven, so don't be alarmed if they are darker than you're used to. They will still taste great.

Let cool on a wire rack before serving.

Oat Bran Muffins

Prep time: 10 minutes | Cook time: 10 to 12 minutes per batch | Makes 8 muffins

160 ml oat bran
120 ml flour
60 ml brown sugar
1 teaspoon baking powder
½ teaspoon baking soda
⅛ teaspoon salt
120 ml buttermilk
1 egg
2 tablespoons rapeseed oil
120 ml chopped dates, raisins, or dried cranberries
24 paper muffin cups
Cooking spray

Preheat the air fryer to 166°C.

In a large bowl, combine the oat bran, flour, brown sugar, baking powder, baking soda, and salt.

In a small bowl, beat together the buttermilk, egg, and oil.

Pour buttermilk mixture into bowl with dry ingredients and stir just until moistened. Do not beat.

Gently stir in dried fruit.

Use triple baking cups to help muffins hold shape during baking. Spray them with cooking spray, place 4 sets of cups in air fryer basket at a time, and fill each one ¾ full of batter.

Cook for 10 to 12 minutes, until top springs back when lightly touched and toothpick inserted in center comes out clean.

Repeat for remaining muffins.

Onion Omelette

Prep time: 10 minutes | Cook time: 12 minutes | Serves 2

3 eggs
Salt and ground black pepper, to taste
½ teaspoons soy sauce
1 large onion, chopped
2 tablespoons grated Cheddar cheese
Cooking spray

Preheat the air fryer to 180°C.

In a bowl, whisk together the eggs, salt, pepper, and soy sauce.

Spritz a small pan with cooking spray. Spread the chopped onion across the bottom of the pan, then transfer the pan to the air fryer. Bake in the preheated air fryer for 6 minutes or until the onion is translucent.

Add the egg mixture on top of the onions to coat well. Add the cheese on top, then continue baking for another 6 minutes.

Allow to cool before serving.

Three-Berry Dutch Pancake

Prep time: 10 minutes | Cook time: 12 to 16 minutes | Serves 4

2 egg whites

1 egg

120 ml wholemeal plain flour plus 1 tablespoon cornflour

120 ml semi-skimmed milk

1 teaspoon pure vanilla extract

1 tablespoon unsalted butter, melted

235 ml sliced fresh strawberries

120 ml fresh blueberries

120 ml fresh raspberries

In a medium bowl, use an eggbeater or hand mixer to quickly mix the egg whites, egg, flour, milk, and vanilla until well combined.

Use a pastry brush to grease the bottom of a baking pan with the melted butter. Immediately pour in the batter and put the basket back in the fryer. Bake at 166°C for 12 to 16 minutes, or until the pancake is puffed and golden brown.

Remove the pan from the air fryer; the pancake will fall. Top with the strawberries, blueberries, and raspberries. Serve immediately.

Turkey Sausage Breakfast Pizza

Prep time: 15 minutes | Cook time: 24 minutes | Serves 2

4 large eggs, divided

1 tablespoon water

½ teaspoon garlic powder

½ teaspoon onion granules

½ teaspoon dried oregano

2 tablespoons coconut flour

3 tablespoons grated Parmesan cheese

120 ml shredded low-moisture Mozzarella or other melting cheese

1 link cooked turkey sausage, chopped (about 60 g)

2 sun-dried tomatoes, finely chopped

2 sping onions, thinly sliced

Preheat the air fryer to 204°C. Line a cake pan with parchment paper and lightly coat the paper with olive oil.

In a large bowl, whisk 2 of the eggs with the water, garlic powder, onion granules, and dried oregano. Add the coconut flour, breaking up any lumps with your hands as you add it to the bowl. Stir the coconut flour into the egg mixture, mixing until smooth. Stir in the Parmesan cheese. Allow the mixture to rest for a few minutes until thick and dough-like.

Transfer the mixture to the prepared pan. Use a spatula to spread it evenly and slightly up the sides of the pan. Air fry until the crust is set but still light in color, about 10 minutes. Top with the cheeses, sausage, and sun-dried tomatoes.

Break the remaining 2 eggs into a small bowl, then slide them onto the pizza. Return the pizza to the air fryer. Air fry 10 to 14 minutes until the egg whites are set and the yolks are the desired doneness. Top with the scallions and allow to rest for 5 minutes before serving.

Quesadillas

Prep time: 10 minutes | Cook time: 15 minutes | Serves 4

4 eggs

2 tablespoons skimmed milk

Salt and pepper, to taste

Oil for misting or cooking spray

4 flour tortillas

4 tablespoons salsa

60 g Cheddar cheese, grated

½ small avocado, peeled and thinly sliced

Preheat the air fryer to 132°C.

Beat together eggs, milk, salt, and pepper.

Spray a baking pan lightly with cooking spray and add egg mixture. Bake for 8 to 9 minutes, stirring every 1 to 2 minutes, until eggs are scrambled to your liking. Remove and set aside.

Spray one side of each tortilla with oil or cooking spray. Flip over. Divide eggs, salsa, cheese, and avocado among the tortillas, covering only half of each tortilla.

Fold each tortilla in half and press down lightly.

Place 2 tortillas in air fryer basket and air fry at 200°C for 3 minutes or until cheese melts and outside feels slightly crispy. Repeat with remaining two tortillas.

Cut each cooked tortilla into halves or thirds.

Baked Peach Oatmeal

Prep time: 5 minutes | Cook time: 30 minutes | Serves 6

Olive oil cooking spray

475 ml certified gluten-free rolled oats

475 ml unsweetened almond milk

60 ml honey, plus more for drizzling (optional)

120 ml non-fat plain Greek yoghurt

1 teaspoon vanilla extract

½ teaspoon ground cinnamon

¼ teaspoon salt

350 ml diced peaches, divided, plus more for serving (optional)

Preheat the air fryer to 192°C. Lightly coat the inside of a 6-inch cake pan with olive oil cooking spray.

In a large bowl, mix together the oats, almond milk, honey, yoghurt, vanilla, cinnamon, and salt until well combined.

Fold in 180 ml peaches and then pour the mixture into the prepared cake pan.

Sprinkle the remaining peaches across the top of the oatmeal mixture. Bake in the air fryer for 30 minutes.

Allow to set and cool for 5 minutes before serving with additional fresh fruit and honey for drizzling, if desired.

Egg and Bacon Muffins

Prep time: 5 minutes | Cook time: 15 minutes | Serves 1

2 eggs

Salt and ground black pepper, to taste

1 tablespoon green pesto

85 g shredded Cheddar cheese

140 g cooked bacon

1 spring onion, chopped

Preheat the air fryer to 176ºC. Line a cupcake tin with parchment paper.

Beat the eggs with pepper, salt, and pesto in a bowl. Mix in the cheese.

Pour the eggs into the cupcake tin and top with the bacon and spring onion.

Bake in the preheated air fryer for 15 minutes, or until the egg is set.

Serve immediately.

Homemade Cherry Breakfast Tarts

Prep time: 15 minutes | Cook time: 20 minutes | Serves 6

Tarts:

2 refrigerated piecrusts

80 ml cherry preserves

1 teaspoon cornflour

Cooking oil

Frosting:

120 ml vanilla yoghurt

30 g cream cheese

1 teaspoon stevia

Rainbow sprinkles

Make the Tarts Place the piecrusts on a flat surface. Using a knife or pizza cutter, cut each piecrust into 3 rectangles, for 6 total. (I discard the unused dough left from slicing the edges.)

In a small bowl, combine the preserves and cornflour. Mix well.

Scoop 1 tablespoon of the preserves mixture onto the top half of each piece of piecrust.

Fold the bottom of each piece up to close the tart. Using the back of a fork, press along the edges of each tart to seal.

Spray the breakfast tarts with cooking oil and place them in the air fryer. I do not recommend stacking the breakfast tarts. They will stick together if stacked. You may need to prepare them in two batches. Bake at 375ºF for 10 minutes.

Allow the breakfast tarts to cool fully before removing from the air fryer.

If necessary, repeat steps 5 and 6 for the remaining breakfast tarts. Make the Frosting

In a small bowl, combine the yoghurt, cream cheese, and stevia. Mix well.

Spread the breakfast tarts with frosting and top with sprinkles, and serve.

Green Eggs and Ham

Prep time: 5 minutes | Cook time: 10 minutes | Serves 2

1 large Hass avocado, halved and pitted

2 thin slices ham

2 large eggs

2 tablespoons chopped spring

onions, plus more for garnish

½ teaspoon fine sea salt

¼ teaspoon ground black pepper

60 ml shredded Cheddar cheese (omit for dairy-free)

Preheat the air fryer to 204ºC.

Place a slice of ham into the cavity of each avocado half. Crack an egg on top of the ham, then sprinkle on the green onions, salt, and pepper.

Place the avocado halves in the air fryer cut side up and air fry for 10 minutes, or until the egg is cooked to your desired doneness. Top with the cheese (if using) and air fry for 30 seconds more, or until the cheese is melted. Garnish with chopped green onions.

Best served fresh. Store extras in an airtight container in the fridge for up to 4 days. Reheat in a preheated 176ºC air fryer for a few minutes, until warmed through.

Potatoes Lyonnaise

Prep time: 10 minutes | Cook time: 31 minutes | Serves 4

1 sweet/mild onion, sliced

1 teaspoon butter, melted

1 teaspoon brown sugar

2 large white potatoes (about 450 g in total), sliced ½-inch

thick

1 tablespoon vegetable oil

Salt and freshly ground black pepper, to taste

Preheat the air fryer to 188ºC.

Toss the sliced onions, melted butter and brown sugar together in the air fryer basket. Air fry for 8 minutes, shaking the basket occasionally to help the onions cook evenly.

While the onions are cooking, bring a saucepan of salted water to a boil on the stovetop. Par-cook the potatoes in boiling water for 3 minutes. Drain the potatoes and pat them dry with a clean kitchen towel.

Add the potatoes to the onions in the air fryer basket and drizzle with vegetable oil. Toss to coat the potatoes with the oil and season with salt and freshly ground black pepper.

Increase the air fryer temperature to 204ºC and air fry for 20 minutes, tossing the vegetables a few times during the cooking time to help the potatoes brown evenly.

Season with salt and freshly ground black pepper and serve warm.

Cauliflower Avocado Toast

Prep time: 15 minutes | Cook time: 8 minutes | Serves 2

1 (40 g) steamer bag cauliflower
1 large egg
120 ml shredded Mozzarella cheese
1 ripe medium avocado
½ teaspoon garlic powder
¼ teaspoon ground black pepper

Cook cauliflower according to package instructions. Remove from bag and place into cheesecloth or clean towel to remove excess moisture.

Place cauliflower into a large bowl and mix in egg and Mozzarella.

Cut a piece of parchment to fit your air fryer basket. Separate the cauliflower mixture into two, and place it on the parchment in two mounds. Press out the cauliflower mounds into a ¼-inch-thick rectangle. Place the parchment into the air fryer basket.

Adjust the temperature to 204ºC and set the timer for 8 minutes.

Flip the cauliflower halfway through the cooking time.

When the timer beeps, remove the parchment and allow the cauliflower to cool 5 minutes.

Cut open the avocado and remove the pit. Scoop out the inside, place it in a medium bowl, and mash it with garlic powder and pepper. Spread onto the cauliflower. Serve immediately.

Spinach and Mushroom Mini Quiche

Prep time: 10 minutes | Cook time: 15 minutes | Serves 4

1 teaspoon olive oil, plus more for spraying
235 ml coarsely chopped mushrooms
235 ml fresh baby spinach, shredded
4 eggs, beaten
120 ml shredded Cheddar cheese
120 ml shredded Mozzarella cheese
¼ teaspoon salt
¼ teaspoon black pepper

Spray 4 silicone baking cups with olive oil and set aside.

In a medium sauté pan over medium heat, warm 1 teaspoon of olive oil. Add the mushrooms and sauté until soft, 3 to 4 minutes.

Add the spinach and cook until wilted, 1 to 2 minutes. Set aside.

In a medium bowl, whisk together the eggs, Cheddar cheese, Mozzarella cheese, salt, and pepper.

Gently fold the mushrooms and spinach into the egg mixture.

Pour ¼ of the mixture into each silicone baking cup.

Place the baking cups into the air fryer basket and air fry at 176ºC for 5 minutes. Stir the mixture in each ramekin slightly and air fry until the egg has set, an additional 3 to 5 minutes.

Italian Egg Cups

Prep time: 5 minutes | Cook time: 10 minutes | Serves 4

Olive oil
235 ml marinara sauce
4 eggs
4 tablespoons shredded Mozzarella cheese
4 teaspoons grated Parmesan cheese
Salt and freshly ground black pepper, to taste
Chopped fresh basil, for garnish

Lightly spray 4 individual ramekins with olive oil.

Pour 60 ml marinara sauce into each ramekin.

Crack one egg into each ramekin on top of the marinara sauce.

Sprinkle 1 tablespoon of Mozzarella and 1 tablespoon of Parmesan on top of each egg. Season with salt and pepper.

Cover each ramekin with aluminum foil. Place two of the ramekins in the air fryer basket.

Air fry at 176ºC for 5 minutes and remove the aluminum foil. Air fry until the top is lightly browned and the egg white is cooked, another 2 to 4 minutes. If you prefer the yolk to be firmer, cook for 3 to 5 more minutes.

Repeat with the remaining two ramekins. Garnish with basil and serve.

Sausage Stuffed Peppers

Prep time: 15 minutes | Cook time: 15 minutes | Serves 4

230 g spicy pork sausage meat, removed from casings
4 large eggs
110 g full-fat cream cheese, softened
60 ml tinned diced tomatoes,
drained
4 green peppers
8 tablespoons shredded chilli cheese
120 ml full-fat sour cream

In a medium skillet over medium heat, crumble and brown the sausage meat until no pink remains. Remove sausage and drain the fat from the pan. Crack eggs into the pan, scramble, and cook until no longer runny.

Place cooked sausage in a large bowl and fold in cream cheese. Mix in diced tomatoes. Gently fold in eggs.

Cut a 4-inch to 5-inch slit in the top of each pepper, removing the seeds and white membrane with a small knife. Separate the filling into four servings and spoon carefully into each pepper. Top each with 2 tablespoons cheese.

Place each pepper into the air fryer basket.

Adjust the temperature to 176ºC and set the timer for 15 minutes.

Peppers will be soft and cheese will be browned when ready. Serve immediately with sour cream on top.

Butternut Squash and Ricotta Frittata

Prep time: 10 minutes | Cook time: 33 minutes | Serves 2 to 3

235 ml cubed (½-inch) butternut squash (160 g)
2 tablespoons olive oil
Coarse or flaky salt and freshly ground black pepper, to taste
4 fresh sage leaves, thinly sliced
6 large eggs, lightly beaten
120 ml ricotta cheese
Cayenne pepper

In a bowl, toss the squash with the olive oil and season with salt and black pepper until evenly coated. Sprinkle the sage on the bottom of a cake pan and place the squash on top. Place the pan in the air fryer and bake at 204ºC for 10 minutes. Stir to incorporate the sage, then cook until the squash is tender and lightly caramelized at the edges, about 3 minutes more.

Pour the eggs over the squash, dollop the ricotta all over, and sprinkle with cayenne. Bake at 150ºC until the eggs are set and the frittata is golden brown on top, about 20 minutes. Remove the pan from the air fryer and cut the frittata into wedges to serve.

Nutty Granola

Prep time: 5 minutes | Cook time: 1 hour | Serves 4

120 ml pecans, coarsely chopped
120 ml walnuts or almonds, coarsely chopped
60 ml desiccated coconut
60 ml almond flour
60 ml ground flaxseed or chia seeds
2 tablespoons sunflower seeds
2 tablespoons melted butter
60 ml granulated sweetener
½ teaspoon ground cinnamon
½ teaspoon vanilla extract
¼ teaspoon ground nutmeg
¼ teaspoon salt
2 tablespoons water

Preheat the air fryer to 120ºC. Cut a piece of parchment paper to fit inside the air fryer basket.

In a large bowl, toss the nuts, coconut, almond flour, ground flaxseed or chia seeds, sunflower seeds, butter, sweetener, cinnamon, vanilla, nutmeg, salt, and water until thoroughly combined.

Spread the granola on the parchment paper and flatten to an even thickness.

Air fry for about an hour, or until golden throughout. Remove from the air fryer and allow to fully cool. Break the granola into bite-size pieces and store in a covered container for up to a week.

Not-So-English Muffins

Prep time: 5 minutes | Cook time: 10 minutes | Serves 4

2 strips turkey bacon, cut in half crosswise
2 whole-grain English muffins, split
235 ml fresh baby spinach, long stems removed
¼ ripe pear, peeled and thinly sliced
4 slices low-moisture Mozzarella or other melting cheese

Place bacon strips in air fryer basket and air fry at 200ºC for 2 minutes. Check and separate strips if necessary so they cook evenly. Cook for 3 to 4 more minutes, until crispy. Remove and drain on paper towels.

Place split muffin halves in air fryer basket and cook for 2 minutes, just until lightly browned.

Open air fryer and top each muffin with a quarter of the baby spinach, several pear slices, a strip of bacon, and a slice of cheese. Air fry at 182ºC for 1 to 2 minutes, until cheese completely melts.

Hole in One

Prep time: 5 minutes | Cook time: 6 to 7 minutes | Serves 1

1 slice bread
1 teaspoon soft butter
1 egg
Salt and pepper, to taste
1 tablespoon shredded Cheddar cheese
2 teaspoons diced ham

Place a baking dish inside air fryer basket and preheat the air fryer to 166ºC.

Using a 2½-inch-diameter biscuit cutter, cut a hole in center of bread slice.

Spread softened butter on both sides of bread.

Lay bread slice in baking dish and crack egg into the hole. Sprinkle egg with salt and pepper to taste.

Cook for 5 minutes.

Turn toast over and top it with shredded cheese and diced ham.

Cook for 1 to 2 more minutes or until yolk is done to your liking.

Chapter 3 Family Favorites

Chapter 3 Family Favorites

Mixed Berry Crumble

Prep time: 10 minutes | Cook time: 11 to 16 minutes | Serves 4

120 ml chopped fresh strawberries
120 ml fresh blueberries
80 ml frozen raspberries
1 tablespoon freshly squeezed lemon juice

1 tablespoon honey
160 ml wholemeal pastry flour
3 tablespoons packed brown sugar
2 tablespoons unsalted butter, melted

In a baking pan, combine the strawberries, blueberries, and raspberries. Drizzle with the lemon juice and honey.

In a small bowl, mix the pastry flour and brown sugar. Stir in the butter and mix until crumbly. Sprinkle this mixture over the fruit.

Bake at 192ºC for 11 to 16 minutes, or until the fruit is tender and bubbly and the topping is golden brown.

Serve warm.

Puffed Egg Tarts

Prep time: 10 minutes | Cook time: 42 minutes | Makes 4 tarts

Oil, for spraying
Plain flour, for dusting
1 (340 g) sheet frozen puff pastry, thawed
180 ml shredded Cheddar cheese, divided

4 large eggs
2 teaspoons chopped fresh parsley
Salt and freshly ground black pepper, to taste

Preheat the air fryer to 200ºC.

Line the air fryer basket with parchment and spray lightly with oil.

Lightly dust your work surface with flour. Unfold the puff pastry and cut it into 4 equal squares.

Place 2 squares in the prepared basket. Cook for 10 minutes. Remove the basket.

Press the centre of each tart shell with a spoon to make an indentation. Sprinkle 3 tablespoons of cheese into each indentation and crack 1 egg into the centre of each tart shell.

Cook for another 7 to 11 minutes, or until the eggs are cooked to your desired doneness.

Repeat with the remaining puff pastry squares, cheese, and eggs.

Sprinkle evenly with the parsley, and season with salt and black pepper. Serve immediately.

Coconut Chicken Tenders

Prep time: 10 minutes | Cook time: 12 minutes | Serves 4

Oil, for spraying
2 large eggs
60 ml milk
1 tablespoon hot sauce
350 ml sweetened flaked or desiccated coconut

180 ml panko breadcrumbs
1 teaspoon salt
½ teaspoon freshly ground black pepper
450 g chicken tenders

Line the air fryer basket with parchment and spray lightly with oil.

In a small bowl, whisk together the eggs, milk, and hot sauce.

In a shallow dish, mix together the coconut, breadcrumbs, salt, and black pepper.

Coat the chicken in the egg mix, then dredge in the coconut mixture until evenly coated.

Place the chicken in the prepared basket and spray liberally with oil.

Air fry at 204ºC for 6 minutes, flip, spray with more oil, and cook for another 6 minutes, or until the internal temperature reaches 74ºC.

Old Bay Tilapia

Prep time: 15 minutes | Cook time: 6 minutes | Serves 4

Oil, for spraying
235 ml panko breadcrumbs
2 tablespoons Old Bay or all-purpose seasoning
2 teaspoons granulated garlic
1 teaspoon onion powder

½ teaspoon salt
¼ teaspoon freshly ground black pepper
1 large egg
4 tilapia fillets

Preheat the air fryer to 204ºC.

Line the air fryer basket with parchment and spray lightly with oil.

In a shallow bowl, mix together the breadcrumbs, seasoning, garlic, onion powder, salt, and black pepper. In a small bowl, whisk the egg. Coat the tilapia in the egg, then dredge in the bread crumb mixture until completely coated.

Place the tilapia in the prepared basket. You may need to work in batches, depending on the size of your air fryer. Spray lightly with oil. Cook for 4 to 6 minutes, depending on the thickness of the fillets, until the internal temperature reaches 64ºC.

Serve immediately.

Beef Jerky

Prep time: 30 minutes | Cook time: 2 hours | Serves 8

Oil, for spraying
450 g silverside steak, cut into thin, short slices
60 ml soy sauce
3 tablespoons packed light

brown sugar
1 tablespoon minced garlic
1 teaspoon ground ginger
1 tablespoon water

Line the air fryer basket with parchment and spray lightly with oil.
Place the steak, soy sauce, brown sugar, garlic, ginger, and water in a zip-top plastic bag, seal, and shake well until evenly coated.
Refrigerate for 30 minutes.
Place the steak in the prepared basket in a single layer. You may need to work in batches, depending on the size of your air fryer.
Air fry at 82ºC for at least 2 hours. Add more time if you like your jerky a bit tougher.

Cheesy Roasted Sweet Potatoes

Prep time: 7 minutes | Cook time: 18 to 23 minutes | Serves 4

2 large sweet potatoes, peeled and sliced
1 teaspoon olive oil
1 tablespoon white balsamic

vinegar
1 teaspoon dried thyme
60 ml grated Parmesan cheese

In a large bowl, drizzle the sweet potato slices with the olive oil and toss.
Sprinkle with the balsamic vinegar and thyme and toss again.
Sprinkle the potatoes with the Parmesan cheese and toss to coat.
Roast the slices, in batches, in the air fryer basket at 204ºC for 18 to 23 minutes, tossing the sweet potato slices in the basket once during cooking, until tender.
Repeat with the remaining sweet potato slices.
Serve immediately.

Bacon-Wrapped Hot Dogs

Prep time: 5 minutes | Cook time: 10 minutes | Serves 4

Oil, for spraying
4 bacon slices
4 beef hot dogs

4 hot dog buns
Toppings of choice

Line the air fryer basket with parchment and spray lightly with oil.
Wrap a strip of bacon tightly around each hot dog, taking care to cover the tips so they don't get too crispy. Secure with a toothpick at each end to keep the bacon from shrinking.

Place the hot dogs in the prepared basket. Air fry at 192ºC for 8 to 9 minutes, depending on how crispy you like the bacon. For extra-crispy, cook the hot dogs at 204ºC for 6 to 8 minutes.
Place the hot dogs in the buns, return them to the air fryer, and cook for another 1 to 2 minutes, or until the buns are warm.
Add your desired toppings and serve.

Cajun Shrimp

Prep time: 15 minutes | Cook time: 9 minutes | Serves 4

Oil, for spraying
450 g jumbo raw shrimp, peeled and deveined
1 tablespoon Cajun seasoning
170 g cooked kielbasa, cut into thick slices
½ medium courgette, cut into ¼-inch-thick slices

½ medium yellow squash or butternut squash, cut into ¼-inch-thick slices
1 green pepper, seeded and cut into 1-inch pieces
2 tablespoons olive oil
½ teaspoon salt

Preheat the air fryer to 204ºC.
Line the air fryer basket with parchment and spray lightly with oil.
In a large bowl, toss together the shrimp and Cajun seasoning. Add the kielbasa, courgette, squash, pepper, olive oil, and salt and mix well.
Transfer the mixture to the prepared basket, taking care not to overcrowd.
You may need to work in batches, depending on the size of your air fryer.
Cook for 9 minutes, shaking and stirring every 3 minutes.
Serve immediately.

Berry Cheesecake

Prep time: 5 minutes | Cook time: 10 minutes | Serves 4

Oil, for spraying
227 g soft white cheese
6 tablespoons sugar
1 tablespoon sour cream

1 large egg
½ teaspoon vanilla extract
¼ teaspoon lemon juice
120 ml fresh mixed berries

Preheat the air fryer to 176ºC.
Line the air fryer basket with parchment and spray lightly with oil.
In a blender, combine the soft white cheese, sugar, sour cream, egg, vanilla, and lemon juice and blend until smooth.
Pour the mixture into a 4-inch springform pan. Place the pan in the prepared basket. Cook for 8 to 10 minutes, or until only the very centre jiggles slightly when the pan is moved.
Refrigerate the cheesecake in the pan for at least 2 hours.
Release the sides from the springform pan, top the cheesecake with the mixed berries, and serve.

Veggie Tuna Melts

Prep time: 15 minutes | Cook time: 7 to 11 minutes | Serves 4

2 low-salt wholemeal English muffins, split
1 (170 g) can chunk light low-salt tuna, drained
235 ml shredded carrot
80 ml chopped mushrooms
2 spring onions, white and green parts, sliced
80 ml fat-free Greek yoghurt
2 tablespoons low-salt wholegrain mustard
2 slices low-salt low-fat Swiss cheese, halved

Place the English muffin halves in the air fryer basket. Air fry at 172ºC for 3 to 4 minutes, or until crisp. Remove from the basket and set aside.

In a medium bowl, thoroughly mix the tuna, carrot, mushrooms, spring onions, yoghurt, and mustard.

Top each half of the muffins with one-fourth of the tuna mixture and a half slice of Swiss cheese.

Air fry for 4 to 7 minutes, or until the tuna mixture is hot and the cheese melts and starts to brown.

Serve immediately.

Apple Pie Egg Rolls

Prep time: 10 minutes | Cook time: 8 minutes | Makes 6 rolls

Oil, for spraying
1 (600 g) can apple pie filling
1 tablespoon plain flour
½ teaspoon lemon juice
¼ teaspoon ground nutmeg
¼ teaspoon ground cinnamon
6 egg roll wrappers

Preheat the air fryer to 204ºC.

Line the air fryer basket with parchment and spray lightly with oil.

In a medium bowl, mix together the pie filling, flour, lemon juice, nutmeg, and cinnamon.

Lay out the egg roll wrappers on a work surface and spoon a dollop of pie filling in the centre of each. Fill a small bowl with water. Dip your finger in the water and, working one at a time, moisten the edges of the wrappers. Fold the wrapper like an envelope (First fold one corner into the centre.

Fold each side corner in, and then fold over the remaining corner, making sure each corner overlaps a bit and the moistened edges stay closed). Use additional water and your fingers to seal any open edges.

Place the rolls in the prepared basket and spray liberally with oil. You may need to work in batches, depending on the size of your air fryer. Cook for 4 minutes, flip, spray with oil, and cook for another 4 minutes, or until crispy and golden brown.

Serve immediately.

Pork Burgers with Red Cabbage Salad

Prep time: 20 minutes | Cook time: 7 to 9 minutes | Serves 4

120 ml Greek yoghurt
2 tablespoons low-salt mustard, divided
1 tablespoon lemon juice
60 ml sliced red cabbage
60 ml grated carrots
450 g lean minced pork
½ teaspoon paprika
235 ml mixed baby lettuce greens
2 small tomatoes, sliced
8 small low-salt wholemeal sandwich buns, cut in half

In a small bowl, combine the yoghurt, 1 tablespoon mustard, lemon juice, cabbage, and carrots; mix and refrigerate.

In a medium bowl, combine the pork, remaining 1 tablespoon mustard, and paprika. Form into 8 small patties.

Put the sliders into the air fryer basket. Air fry at 204ºC for 7 to 9 minutes, or until the sliders register 74ºC as tested with a meat thermometer.

Assemble the burgers by placing some of the lettuce greens on a bun bottom. Top with a tomato slice, the burgers, and the cabbage mixture. Add the bun top and serve immediately.

Fried Green Tomatoes

Prep time: 15 minutes | Cook time: 6 to 8 minutes | Serves 4

4 medium green tomatoes
80 ml plain flour
2 egg whites
60 ml almond milk
235 ml ground almonds
120 ml panko breadcrumbs
2 teaspoons olive oil
1 teaspoon paprika
1 clove garlic, minced

Rinse the tomatoes and pat dry. Cut the tomatoes into ½-inch slices, discarding the thinner ends.

Put the flour on a plate.

In a shallow bowl, beat the egg whites with the almond milk until frothy.

And on another plate, combine the almonds, breadcrumbs, olive oil, paprika, and garlic and mix well.

Dip the tomato slices into the flour, then into the egg white mixture, then into the almond mixture to coat.

Place four of the coated tomato slices in the air fryer basket. Air fry at 204ºC for 6 to 8 minutes or until the tomato coating is crisp and golden brown.

Repeat with remaining tomato slices and serve immediately.

Steak Tips and Potatoes

Oil, for spraying

227 g baby gold potatoes, cut in half

½ teaspoon salt

450 g steak, cut into ½-inch pieces

1 teaspoon Worcestershire sauce

1 teaspoon granulated garlic

½ teaspoon salt

½ teaspoon freshly ground black pepper

Line the air fryer basket with parchment and spray lightly with oil.

In a microwave-safe bowl, combine the potatoes and salt, then pour in about ½ inch of water.

Microwave for 7 minutes, or until the potatoes are nearly tender. Drain.

In a large bowl, gently mix together the steak, potatoes, Worcestershire sauce, garlic, salt, and black pepper.

Spread the mixture in an even layer in the prepared basket. Air fry at 204°C for 12 to 17 minutes, stirring after 5 to 6 minutes. The cooking time will depend on the thickness of the meat and preferred doneness.

Meringue Cookies

Oil, for spraying

4 large egg whites

235 ml sugar

Pinch cream of tartar

Preheat the air fryer to 60°C.

Line the air fryer basket with parchment and spray lightly with oil.

In a small heatproof bowl, whisk together the egg whites and sugar.

Fill a small saucepan halfway with water, place it over medium heat, and bring to a light simmer.

Place the bowl with the egg whites on the saucepan, making sure the bottom of the bowl does not touch the water.

Whisk the mixture until the sugar is dissolved. Transfer the mixture to a large bowl and add the cream of tartar.

Using an electric mixer, beat the mixture on high until it is glossy and stiff peaks form. Transfer the mixture to a piping bag or a zip-top plastic bag with a corner cut off.

Pipe rounds into the prepared basket. You may need to work in batches, depending on the size of your air fryer. Cook for 1 hour 30 minutes.

Turn off the air fryer and let the meringues cool completely inside. The residual heat will continue to dry them out.

Chapter 4 Holiday Specials

Chapter 4 Holiday Specials

Lemony and Garlicky Asparagus

Prep time: 5 minutes | Cook time: 10 minutes | Makes 10 spears

10 spears asparagus (about 230 g in total), snap the ends off
1 tablespoon lemon juice
2 teaspoons minced garlic
½ teaspoon salt
¼ teaspoon ground black pepper
Cooking spray

Preheat the air fryer to 204°C.
Line a parchment paper in the air fryer basket.
Put the asparagus spears in a large bowl. Drizzle with lemon juice and sprinkle with minced garlic, salt, and ground black pepper. Toss to coat well.
Transfer the asparagus in the preheated air fryer and spritz with cooking spray. Air fryer for 10 minutes or until wilted and soft. Flip the asparagus halfway through.
Serve immediately.

Shrimp with Sriracha and Worcestershire Sauce

Prep time: 15 minutes | Cook time: 10 minutes per batch | Serves 4

1 tablespoon Sriracha sauce
1 teaspoon Worcestershire sauce
2 tablespoons sweet chilli sauce
180 ml mayonnaise
1 egg, beaten
235 ml panko breadcrumbs
450 g raw shrimp, shelled and deveined, rinsed and drained
Lime wedges, for serving
Cooking spray

Preheat the air fryer to 182°C. Spritz the air fryer basket with cooking spray.
Combine the Sriracha sauce, Worcestershire sauce, chilli sauce, and mayo in a bowl. Stir to mix well.
Reserve 80 ml the mixture as the dipping sauce.
Combine the remaining sauce mixture with the beaten egg. Stir to mix well.
Put the panko in a separate bowl.
Dredge the shrimp in the sauce mixture first, then into the panko. Roll the shrimp to coat well. Shake the excess off.
Place the shrimp in the preheated air fryer, then spritz with cooking spray. You may need to work in batches to avoid overcrowding.
Air fry the shrimp for 10 minutes or until opaque. Flip the shrimp halfway through the cooking time.
Remove the shrimp from the air fryer and serve with reserve sauce mixture and squeeze the lime wedges over.

Garlicky Knots with Parsley

Prep time: 10 minutes | Cook time: 10 minutes | Makes 8 knots

1 teaspoon dried parsley
60 ml melted butter
2 teaspoons garlic powder
1 (312 g) tube refrigerated French bread dough, cut into 8 slices

Preheat the air fryer to 176°C.
Combine the parsley, butter, and garlic powder in a bowl. Stir to mix well.
Place the French bread dough slices on a clean work surface, then roll each slice into a 6-inch-long rope. Tie the ropes into knots and arrange them on a plate. Brush the knots with butter mixture.
Transfer the knots into the air fryer. You need to work in batches to avoid overcrowding. Air fry for 5 minutes or until the knots are golden brown. Flip the knots halfway through the cooking time.
Serve immediately.

Parsnip Fries with Garlic-Yoghurt Dip

Prep timeParsnip Fries with Garlic-Yoghurt Dip

3 medium parsnips, peeled, cut into sticks
¼ teaspoon rock salt
1 teaspoon olive oil
1 garlic clove, unpeeled
Cooking spray
Dip:
60 ml plain Greek yoghurt
⅛ teaspoon garlic powder
1 tablespoon sour cream
¼ teaspoon rock salt
Freshly ground black pepper, to taste

Preheat the air fryer to 182°C. Spritz the air fryer basket with cooking spray.
Put the parsnip sticks in a large bowl, then sprinkle with salt and drizzle with olive oil.
Transfer the parsnip into the preheated air fryer and add the garlic. Air fry for 5 minutes, then remove the garlic from the air fryer and shake the basket. Air fry for 5 more minutes or until the parsnip sticks are crisp.
Meanwhile, peel the garlic and crush it.
Combine the crushed garlic with the ingredients for the dip. Stir to mix well.
When the frying is complete, remove the parsnip fries from the air fryer and serve with the dipping sauce.

South Carolina Shrimp and Corn Bake

Prep time: 10 minutes | Cook time: 18 minutes | Serves 2

1 ear corn, husk and silk removed, cut into 2-inch rounds
227 g red potatoes, unpeeled, cut into 1-inch pieces
2 teaspoons Old Bay or all-purpose seasoning, divided
2 teaspoons vegetable oil, divided
¼ teaspoon ground black pepper
227 g large shrimps (about 12 shrimps), deveined
170 g andouille or chorizo sausage, cut into 1-inch pieces
2 garlic cloves, minced
1 tablespoon chopped fresh parsley

Preheat the air fryer to 204ºC.
Put the corn rounds and potatoes in a large bowl. Sprinkle with 1 teaspoon of seasoning and drizzle with vegetable oil. Toss to coat well.
Transfer the corn rounds and potatoes on a baking sheet, then put in the preheated air fryer. Bake for 12 minutes or until soft and browned. Shake the basket halfway through the cooking time.
Meanwhile, cut slits into the shrimps but be careful not to cut them through.
Combine the shrimps, sausage, remaining seasoning, and remaining vegetable oil in the large bowl. Toss to coat well.
When the baking of the potatoes and corn rounds is complete, add the shrimps and sausage and bake for 6 more minutes or until the shrimps are opaque. Shake the basket halfway through the cooking time.
When the baking is finished, serve them on a plate and spread with parsley before serving.

Lush Snack Mix

Prep time: 10 minutes | Cook time: 10 minutes | Serves 10

120 ml honey
3 tablespoons butter, melted
1 teaspoon salt
475 ml sesame sticks
475 ml pumpkin seeds
475 ml granola
235 ml cashews
475 ml crispy corn puff cereal
475 ml mini pretzel crisps

In a bowl, combine the honey, butter, and salt.
In another bowl, mix the sesame sticks, pumpkin seeds, granola, cashews, corn puff cereal, and pretzel crisps. Combine the contents of the two bowls.
Preheat the air fryer to 188ºC.
Put the mixture in the air fryer basket and air fry for 10 to 12 minutes to toast the snack mixture, shaking the basket frequently. Do this in two batches.
Put the snack mix on a cookie sheet and allow it to cool fully.
Serve immediately.

Classic Churros

Prep time: 35 minutes | Cook time: 10 minutes per batch | Makes 12 churros

4 tablespoons butter
¼ teaspoon salt
120 ml water
120 ml plain flour
2 large eggs
2 teaspoons ground cinnamon
60 ml granulated white sugar
Cooking spray

Put the butter, salt, and water in a saucepan. Bring to a boil until the butter is melted on high heat. Keep stirring.
Reduce the heat to medium and fold in the flour to form a dough. Keep cooking and stirring until the dough is dried out and coat the pan with a crust.
Turn off the heat and scrape the dough in a large bowl. Allow to cool for 15 minutes.
Break and whisk the eggs into the dough with a hand mixer until the dough is sanity and firm enough to shape. Scoop up 1 tablespoon of the dough and roll it into a ½-inch-diameter and 2-inch-long cylinder.
Repeat with remaining dough to make 12 cylinders in total. Combine the cinnamon and sugar in a large bowl and dunk the cylinders into the cinnamon mix to coat.
Arrange the cylinders on a plate and refrigerate for 20 minutes.
Preheat the air fryer to 192ºC.
Spritz the air fryer basket with cooking spray.
Place the cylinders in batches in the air fryer basket and spritz with cooking spray. Air fry for 10 minutes or until golden brown and fluffy. Flip them halfway through.
Serve immediately.

Frico

Prep time: 5 minutes | Cook time: 5 minutes | Serves 2

235 ml shredded aged Manchego cheese
1 teaspoon plain flour
½ teaspoon cumin seeds
¼ teaspoon cracked black pepper

Preheat the air fryer to 192ºC.
Line the air fryer basket with parchment paper.
Combine the cheese and flour in a bowl. Stir to mix well.
Spread the mixture in the basket into a 4-inch round.
Combine the cumin and black pepper in a small bowl. Stir to mix well.
Sprinkle the cumin mixture over the cheese round.
Air fry 5 minutes or until the cheese is lightly browned and frothy.
Use tongs to transfer the cheese wafer onto a plate and slice to serve.

Simple Air Fried Crispy Brussels Sprouts

Prep time: 5 minutes | Cook time: 20 minutes | Serves 4

¼ teaspoon salt
⅛ teaspoon ground black pepper
1 tablespoon extra-virgin olive oil

450 g Brussels sprouts, trimmed and halved
Lemon wedges, for garnish

Preheat the air fryer to 176°C.

Combine the salt, black pepper, and olive oil in a large bowl. Stir to mix well.

Add the Brussels sprouts to the bowl of mixture and toss to coat well.

Arrange the Brussels sprouts in the preheated air fryer. Air fry for 20 minutes or until lightly browned and wilted. Shake the basket two times during the air frying.

Transfer the cooked Brussels sprouts to a large plate and squeeze the lemon wedges on top to serve.

Whole Chicken Roast

Prep time: 10 minutes | Cook time: 1 hour | Serves 6

1 teaspoon salt
1 teaspoon Italian seasoning
½ teaspoon freshly ground black pepper
½ teaspoon paprika

½ teaspoon garlic powder
½ teaspoon onion powder
2 tablespoons olive oil, plus more as needed
1 (1.8 kg) small chicken

Preheat the air fryer to 182°C. Grease the air fryer basket lightly with olive oil.

In a small bowl, mix the salt, Italian seasoning, pepper, paprika, garlic powder, and onion powder.

Remove any giblets from the chicken. Pat the chicken dry thoroughly with paper towels, including the cavity. Brush the chicken all over with the olive oil and rub it with the seasoning mixture.

Truss the chicken or tie the legs with butcher's twine. This will make it easier to flip the chicken during cooking.

Put the chicken in the air fryer basket, breast-side down. Air fry for 30 minutes. Flip the chicken over and baste it with any drippings collected in the bottom drawer of the air fryer.

Lightly brush the chicken with olive oil. Air fry for 20 minutes.

Flip the chicken over one last time and air fry until a thermometer inserted into the thickest part of the thigh reaches at least 74°C and it's crispy and golden, 10 more minutes.

Continue to cook, checking every 5 minutes until the chicken reaches the correct internal temperature.

Let the chicken rest for 10 minutes before carving and serving.

Classic Poutine

Prep time: 15 minutes | Cook time: 25 minutes | Serves 2

2 russet or Maris Piper potatoes, scrubbed and cut into ½-inch sticks
2 teaspoons vegetable oil
2 tablespoons butter
¼ onion, minced
¼ teaspoon dried thyme
1 clove garlic, smashed

3 tablespoons plain flour
1 teaspoon tomato paste
350 ml beef stock
2 teaspoons Worcestershire sauce
Salt and freshly ground black pepper, to taste
160 ml chopped string cheese

Bring a pot of water to a boil, then put in the potato sticks and blanch for 4 minutes.

Preheat the air fryer to 204°C.

Drain the potato sticks and rinse under running cold water, then pat dry with paper towels.

Transfer the sticks in a large bowl and drizzle with vegetable oil. Toss to coat well.

Place the potato sticks in the preheated air fryer. Air fry for 25 minutes or until the sticks are golden brown. Shake the basket at least three times during the frying.

Meanwhile, make the gravy: Heat the butter in a saucepan over medium heat until melted. Add the onion, thyme, and garlic and sauté for 5 minutes or until the onion is translucent. Add the flour and sauté for an additional 2 minutes.

Pour in the tomato paste and beef stock and cook for 1 more minute or until lightly thickened. Drizzle the gravy with Worcestershire sauce and sprinkle with salt and ground black pepper.

Reduce the heat to low to keep the gravy warm until ready to serve.

Transfer the fried potato sticks onto a plate, then sprinkle with salt and ground black pepper. Scatter with string cheese and pour the gravy over. Serve warm.

Air Fried Blistered Tomatoes

Prep time: 5 minutes | Cook time: 10 minutes | Serves 4 to 6

900 g cherry tomatoes
2 tablespoons olive oil
2 teaspoons balsamic vinegar

½ teaspoon salt
½ teaspoon ground black pepper

Preheat the air fryer with a cake pan to 204°C.

Toss the cherry tomatoes with olive oil in a large bowl to coat well. Pour the tomatoes in the cake pan.

Air fry the cherry tomatoes for 10 minutes or until the tomatoes are blistered and lightly wilted. Shake the basket halfway through.

Transfer the blistered tomatoes to a large bowl and toss with balsamic vinegar, salt, and black pepper before serving.

Classic Latkes

Prep time: 15 minutes | Cook time: 10 minutes | Makes 4 latkes

1 egg

2 tablespoons plain flour

2 medium potatoes, peeled and shredded, rinsed and drained

¼ teaspoon granulated garlic

½ teaspoon salt

Cooking spray

Preheat the air fryer to 192°C. Spritz the air fryer basket with cooking spray.

Whisk together the egg, flour, potatoes, garlic, and salt in a large bowl. Stir to mix well.

Divide the mixture into four parts, then flatten them into four circles.

Arrange the circles into the preheated air fryer.

Spritz the circles with cooking spray, then air fry for 10 minutes or until golden brown and crispy. Flip the latkes halfway through.

Serve immediately.

Garlicky Baked Cherry Tomatoes

Prep time: 5 minutes | Cook time: 4 to 6 minutes | Serves 2

475 ml cherry tomatoes

1 clove garlic, thinly sliced

1 teaspoon olive oil

⅛ teaspoon rock salt

1 tablespoon freshly chopped basil, for topping

Cooking spray

Preheat the air fryer to 182°C.

Spritz the air fryer baking pan with cooking spray and set aside.

In a large bowl, toss together the cherry tomatoes, sliced garlic, olive oil, and rock salt.

Spread the mixture in an even layer in the prepared pan.

Bake in the preheated air fryer for 4 to 6 minutes, or until the tomatoes become soft and wilted.

Transfer to a bowl and rest for 5 minutes.

Top with the chopped basil and serve warm.

Fried Dill Pickles with Buttermilk Dressing

Prep time: 45 minutes | Cook time: 8 minutes | Serves 6 to 8

Buttermilk Dressing:

60 ml buttermilk

60 ml chopped spring onions

180 ml mayonnaise

120 ml sour cream

½ teaspoon cayenne pepper

½ teaspoon onion powder

½ teaspoon garlic powder

1 tablespoon chopped chives

2 tablespoons chopped fresh dill

Rock salt and ground black

pepper, to taste

Fried Dill Pickles:

180 ml plain flour

1 (900 g) jar kosher dill pickles, cut into 4 spears, drained

600 ml panko breadcrumbs

2 eggs, beaten with 2 tablespoons water

Rock salt and ground black pepper, to taste

Cooking spray

Preheat the air fryer to 204°C.

Combine the ingredients for the dressing in a bowl. Stir to mix well.

Wrap the bowl in plastic and refrigerate for 30 minutes or until ready to serve.

Pour the flour in a bowl and sprinkle with salt and ground black pepper. Stir to mix well.

Put the breadcrumbs in a separate bowl. Pour the beaten eggs in a third bowl.

Dredge the pickle spears in the flour, then into the eggs, and then into the panko to coat well. Shake the excess off.

Arrange the pickle spears in a single layer in the preheated air fryer and spritz with cooking spray. Air fry for 8 minutes. Flip the pickle spears halfway through.

Serve the pickle spears with buttermilk dressing.

Chapter 5 Vegetarian Mains

Chapter 5 Vegetarian Mains

Greek Stuffed Aubergine

Prep time: 15 minutes | Cook time: 20 minutes | Serves 2

1 large aubergine	235 ml fresh spinach
2 tablespoons unsalted butter	2 tablespoons diced red pepper
¼ medium brown onion, diced	120 ml crumbled feta
60 ml chopped artichoke hearts	

Slice aubergine in half lengthwise and scoop out flesh, leaving enough inside for shell to remain intact.

Take aubergine that was scooped out, chop it, and set aside.

In a medium skillet over medium heat, add butter and onion. Sauté until onions begin to soften, about 3 to 5 minutes. Add chopped aubergine, artichokes, spinach, and pepper.

Continue cooking 5 minutes until peppers soften and spinach wilts. Remove from the heat and gently fold in the feta.

Place filling into each aubergine shell and place into the air fryer basket. Adjust the temperature to 160ºC and air fry for 20 minutes. Aubergine will be tender when done.

Serve warm.

Broccoli-Cheese Fritters

Prep time: 5 minutes | Cook time: 20 to 25 minutes | Serves 4

235 ml broccoli florets	1 teaspoon garlic powder
235 ml shredded Mozzarella cheese	Salt and freshly ground black pepper, to taste
180 ml almond flour	2 eggs, lightly beaten
120 ml milled flaxseed, divided	120 ml ranch dressing
2 teaspoons baking powder	

Preheat the air fryer to 204ºC.

In a food processor fitted with a metal blade, pulse the broccoli until very finely chopped.

Transfer the broccoli to a large bowl and add the Mozzarella, almond flour, 60 ml milled flaxseed, baking powder, and garlic powder. Stir until thoroughly combined. Season to taste with salt and black pepper.

Add the eggs and stir again to form a sticky dough. Shape the dough into 1¼-inch fritters.

Place the remaining 60 ml milled flaxseed in a shallow bowl and roll the fritters in the meal to form an even coating.

Working in batches if necessary, arrange the fritters in a single layer in the basket of the air fryer and spray generously with olive oil. Pausing halfway through the cooking time to shake the basket, air fry for 20 to 25 minutes until the fritters are golden brown and crispy.

Serve with the ranch dressing for dipping.

Roasted Vegetables with Rice

Prep time: 5 minutes | Cook time: 12 minutes | Serves 4

2 teaspoons melted butter	1 red onion, chopped
235 ml chopped mushrooms	1 garlic clove, minced
235 ml cooked rice	Salt and black pepper, to taste
235 ml peas	2 hard-boiled eggs, grated
1 carrot, chopped	1 tablespoon soy sauce

Preheat the air fryer to 192ºC.

Coat a baking dish with melted butter.

Stir together the mushrooms, cooked rice, peas, carrot, onion, garlic, salt, and pepper in a large bowl until well mixed.

Pour the mixture into the prepared baking dish and transfer to the air fryer basket.

Roast in the preheated air fryer for 12 minutes until the vegetables are tender. Divide the mixture among four plates.

Serve warm with a sprinkle of grated eggs and a drizzle of soy sauce.

Tangy Asparagus and Broccoli

Prep time: 25 minutes | Cook time: 22 minutes | Serves 4

230 g asparagus, cut into 1½-inch pieces	Salt and white pepper, to taste
230 g broccoli, cut into 1½-inch pieces	120 ml vegetable broth
2 tablespoons olive oil	2 tablespoons apple cider vinegar

Place the vegetables in a single layer in the lightly greased air fryer basket. Drizzle the olive oil over the vegetables. Sprinkle with salt and white pepper. Cook at 192ºC for 15 minutes, shaking the basket halfway through the cooking time.

Add 120 ml of vegetable broth to a saucepan; bring to a rapid boil and add the vinegar. Cook for 5 to 7 minutes or until the sauce has reduced by half.

Spoon the sauce over the warm vegetables and serve immediately. Bon appétit!

Spinach-Artichoke Stuffed Mushrooms

Prep time: 10 minutes | Cook time: 10 to 14 minutes | Serves 4

2 tablespoons olive oil
4 large portobello mushrooms, stems removed and gills scraped out
½ teaspoon salt
¼ teaspoon freshly ground pepper
110 g goat cheese, crumbled

120 ml chopped marinated artichoke hearts
235 ml frozen spinach, thawed and squeezed dry
120 ml grated Parmesan cheese
2 tablespoons chopped fresh parsley

Preheat the air fryer to 204°C.

Rub the olive oil over the portobello mushrooms until thoroughly coated. Sprinkle both sides with the salt and black pepper. Place top-side down on a clean work surface.

In a small bowl, combine the goat cheese, artichoke hearts, and spinach. Mash with the back of a fork until thoroughly combined. Divide the cheese mixture among the mushrooms and sprinkle with the Parmesan cheese.

Air fry for 10 to 14 minutes until the mushrooms are tender and the cheese has begun to brown.

Top with the fresh parsley just before serving.

Almond-Cauliflower Gnocchi

Prep time: 5 minutes | Cook time: 25 to 30 minutes | Serves 4

1.2 L cauliflower florets
160 ml almond flour
½ teaspoon salt

60 ml unsalted butter, melted
60 ml grated Parmesan cheese

In a food processor fitted with a metal blade, pulse the cauliflower until finely chopped.

Transfer the cauliflower to a large microwave-safe bowl and cover it with a paper towel. Microwave for 5 minutes.

Spread the cauliflower on a towel to cool. When cool enough to handle, draw up the sides of the towel and squeeze tightly over a sink to remove the excess moisture.

Return the cauliflower to the food processor and whirl until creamy. Sprinkle in the flour and salt and pulse until a sticky dough comes together. Transfer the dough to a workspace lightly floured with almond flour.

Shape the dough into a ball and divide into 4 equal sections. Roll each section into a rope 1 inch thick. Slice the dough into squares with a sharp knife.

Preheat the air fryer to 204°C.

Working in batches if necessary, place the gnocchi in a single layer in the basket of the air fryer and spray generously with olive oil.

Pausing halfway through the cooking time to turn the gnocchi, air fry for 25 to 30 minutes until golden brown and crispy on the edges.

Transfer to a large bowl and toss with the melted butter and Parmesan cheese.

Vegetable Burgers

Prep time: 10 minutes | Cook time: 12 minutes | Serves 4

227 g cremini or chestnut mushrooms
2 large egg yolks
½ medium courgette, trimmed and chopped
60 ml peeled and chopped

brown onion
1 clove garlic, peeled and finely minced
½ teaspoon salt
¼ teaspoon ground black pepper

Place all ingredients into a food processor and pulse twenty times until finely chopped and combined.

Separate mixture into four equal sections and press each into a burger shape.

Place burgers into ungreased air fryer basket. Adjust the temperature to 192°C and air fry for 12 minutes, turning burgers halfway through cooking. Burgers will be browned and firm when done.

Place burgers on a large plate and let cool 5 minutes before serving.

Potato and Broccoli with Tofu Scramble

Prep time: 15 minutes | Cook time: 30 minutes | Serves 3

600 ml chopped red potato
2 tablespoons olive oil, divided
1 block tofu, chopped finely
2 tablespoons tamari
1 teaspoon turmeric powder

½ teaspoon onion powder
½ teaspoon garlic powder
120 ml chopped onion
1 L broccoli florets

Preheat the air fryer to 204°C.

Toss together the potatoes and 1 tablespoon of the olive oil.

Air fry the potatoes in a baking dish for 15 minutes, shaking once during the cooking time to ensure they fry evenly.

Combine the tofu, the remaining 1 tablespoon of the olive oil, turmeric, onion powder, tamari, and garlic powder together, stirring in the onions, followed by the broccoli.

Top the potatoes with the tofu mixture and air fry for an additional 15 minutes.

Serve warm.

Roasted Veggie Bowl

Prep time: 10 minutes | Cook time: 15 minutes | Serves 2

235 ml broccoli florets
235 ml quartered Brussels sprouts
120 ml cauliflower florets
¼ medium white onion, peeled and sliced ¼ inch thick

½ medium green pepper, seeded and sliced ¼ inch thick
1 tablespoon coconut oil
2 teaspoons chilli powder
½ teaspoon garlic powder
½ teaspoon cumin

Toss all ingredients together in a large bowl until vegetables are fully coated with oil and seasoning.

Pour vegetables into the air fryer basket. Adjust the temperature to 182°C and roast for 15 minutes. Shake two or three times during cooking.

Serve warm.

Spaghetti Squash Alfredo

Prep time: 10 minutes | Cook time: 15 minutes | Serves 2

½ large cooked spaghetti squash
2 tablespoons salted butter, melted
120 ml low-carb Alfredo sauce
60 ml grated vegetarian Parmesan cheese

½ teaspoon garlic powder
1 teaspoon dried parsley
¼ teaspoon ground peppercorn
120 ml shredded Italian blend cheese

Using a fork, remove the strands of spaghetti squash from the shell. Place into a large bowl with butter and Alfredo sauce.

Sprinkle with Parmesan, garlic powder, parsley, and peppercorn. Pour into a 1 L round baking dish and top with shredded cheese.

Place dish into the air fryer basket. Adjust the temperature to 160°C and bake for 15 minutes. When finished, cheese will be golden and bubbling.

Serve immediately.

Stuffed Portobellos

Prep time: 10 minutes | Cook time: 8 minutes | Serves 4

85 g soft white cheese
½ medium courgette, trimmed and chopped
60 ml seeded and chopped red pepper
350 ml chopped fresh spinach

leaves
4 large portobello mushrooms, stems removed
2 tablespoons coconut oil, melted
½ teaspoon salt

In a medium bowl, mix soft white cheese, courgette, pepper, and spinach.

Drizzle mushrooms with coconut oil and sprinkle with salt. Scoop ¼ courgette mixture into each mushroom.

Place mushrooms into ungreased air fryer basket. Adjust the temperature to 204°C and air fry for 8 minutes. Portobellos will be tender, and tops will be browned when done.

Serve warm.

Crispy Fried Okra with Chilli

Prep time: 5 minutes | Cook time: 10 minutes | Serves 4

3 tablespoons sour cream
2 tablespoons flour
2 tablespoons semolina
½ teaspoon red chilli powder

Salt and black pepper, to taste
450 g okra, halved
Cooking spray

Preheat the air fryer to 204°C. Spray the air fryer basket with cooking spray.

In a shallow bowl, place the sour cream. In another shallow bowl, thoroughly combine the flour, semolina, red chilli powder, salt, and pepper.

Dredge the okra in the sour cream, then roll in the flour mixture until evenly coated.

Arrange the okra in the air fryer basket and air fry for 10 minutes, flipping the okra halfway through, or until golden brown and crispy. Cool for 5 minutes before serving.

Herbed Broccoli with Cheese

Prep time: 5 minutes | Cook time: 18 minutes | Serves 4

1 large-sized head broccoli, stemmed and cut into small florets
2½ tablespoons rapeseed oil
2 teaspoons dried basil

2 teaspoons dried rosemary
Salt and ground black pepper, to taste
80 ml grated yellow cheese

Bring a pot of lightly salted water to a boil. Add the broccoli florets to the boiling water and let boil for about 3 minutes.

Drain the broccoli florets well and transfer to a large bowl. Add the rapeseed oil, basil, rosemary, salt, and black pepper to the bowl and toss until the broccoli is fully coated.

Preheat the air fryer to 200°C.

Place the broccoli in the air fryer basket and air fry for about 15 minutes, shaking the basket halfway through, or until the broccoli is crisp.

Serve the broccoli warm with grated cheese sprinkled on top.

Cheesy Cauliflower Pizza Crust

Prep time: 15 minutes | Cook time: 11 minutes | Serves 2

1 (340 g) steamer bag cauliflower	2 tablespoons blanched finely ground almond flour
120 ml shredded extra mature Cheddar cheese	1 teaspoon Italian blend seasoning
1 large egg	

Cook cauliflower according to package instructions.

Remove from bag and place into cheesecloth or paper towel to remove excess water.

Place cauliflower into a large bowl. Add cheese, egg, almond flour, and Italian seasoning to the bowl and mix well.

Cut a piece of parchment to fit your air fryer basket.

Press cauliflower into 6-inch round circle.

Place into the air fryer basket. Adjust the temperature to 182°C and air fry for 11 minutes. After 7 minutes, flip the pizza crust.

Add preferred toppings to pizza. Place back into air fryer basket and cook an additional 4 minutes or until fully cooked and golden. Serve immediately.

Buffalo Cauliflower Bites with Blue Cheese

Prep time: 10 minutes | Cook time: 8 to 10 minutes | Serves 4

1 large head cauliflower, chopped into florets	120 ml mayonnaise
1 tablespoon olive oil	60 ml sour cream
Salt and freshly ground black pepper, to taste	2 tablespoons double cream
	1 tablespoon fresh lemon juice
60 ml unsalted butter, melted	1 clove garlic, minced
60 ml hot sauce	60 ml crumbled blue cheese
Garlic Blue Cheese Dip:	Salt and freshly ground black pepper, to taste

Preheat the air fryer to 204°C.

In a large bowl, combine the cauliflower and olive oil. Season to taste with salt and black pepper. Toss until the vegetables are thoroughly coated.

Working in batches, place half of the cauliflower in the air fryer basket. Pausing halfway through the cooking time to shake the basket, air fry for 8 to 10 minutes until the cauliflower is evenly browned.

Transfer to a large bowl and repeat with the remaining cauliflower. In a small bowl, whisk together the melted butter and hot sauce.

To make the dip: In a small bowl, combine the mayonnaise, sour cream, double cream, lemon juice, garlic, and blue cheese. Season to taste with salt and freshly ground black pepper.

Just before serving, pour the butter mixture over the cauliflower and toss gently until thoroughly coated. Serve with the dip on the side.

Crispy Aubergine Slices with Parsley

Prep time: 5 minutes | Cook time: 10 to 12 minutes | Serves 4

235 ml flour	2 aubergines, sliced
4 eggs	2 garlic cloves, sliced
Salt, to taste	2 tablespoons chopped parsley
475 ml breadcrumbs	Cooking spray
1 teaspoon Italian seasoning	

Preheat the air fryer to 200°C. Spritz the air fryer basket with cooking spray.

On a plate, place the flour. In a shallow bowl, whisk the eggs with salt. In another shallow bowl, combine the breadcrumbs and Italian seasoning.

Dredge the aubergine slices, one at a time, in the flour, then in the whisked eggs, finally in the bread crumb mixture to coat well.

Arrange the coated aubergine slices in the air fryer basket and air fry for 10 to 12 minutes until golden brown and crispy. Flip the aubergine slices halfway through the cooking time.

Transfer the aubergine slices to a plate and sprinkle the garlic and parsley on top before serving.

Pesto Spinach Flatbread

Prep time: 10 minutes | Cook time: 8 minutes | Serves 4

235 ml blanched finely ground almond flour	cheese
60 g soft white cheese	235 ml chopped fresh spinach leaves
475 ml shredded Mozzarella	2 tablespoons basil pesto

Place flour, soft white cheese, and Mozzarella in a large microwave-safe bowl and microwave on high 45 seconds, then stir.

Fold in spinach and microwave an additional 15 seconds. Stir until a soft dough ball forms.

Cut two pieces of parchment paper to fit air fryer basket.

Separate dough into two sections and press each out on ungreased parchment to create 6-inch rounds.

Spread 1 tablespoon pesto over each flatbread and place rounds on parchment into ungreased air fryer basket.

Adjust the temperature to 176°C and air fry for 8 minutes, turning crusts halfway through cooking. Flatbread will be golden when done.

Let cool 5 minutes before slicing and serving.

Cauliflower Rice-Stuffed Peppers

Prep time: 10 minutes | Cook time: 15 minutes | Serves 4

475 ml uncooked cauliflower rice

180 ml drained canned petite diced tomatoes

2 tablespoons olive oil

235 ml shredded Mozzarella cheese

¼ teaspoon salt

¼ teaspoon ground black pepper

4 medium green peppers, tops removed, seeded

In a large bowl, mix all ingredients except peppers. Scoop mixture evenly into peppers.

Place peppers into ungreased air fryer basket. Adjust the temperature to 176ºC and air fry for 15 minutes. Peppers will be tender, and cheese will be melted when done.

Serve warm.

Cheese Stuffed Peppers

Prep time: 20 minutes | Cook time: 15 minutes | Serves 2

1 red pepper, top and seeds removed

1 yellow pepper, top and seeds removed

Salt and pepper, to taste

235 ml Cottage cheese

4 tablespoons mayonnaise

2 pickles, chopped

Arrange the peppers in the lightly greased air fryer basket. Cook in the preheated air fryer at 204ºC for 15 minutes, turning them over halfway through the cooking time.

Season with salt and pepper.

Then, in a mixing bowl, combine the soft white cheese with the mayonnaise and chopped pickles.

Stuff the pepper with the soft white cheese mixture and serve. Enjoy!

Broccoli with Garlic Sauce

Prep time: 19 minutes | Cook time: 15 minutes | Serves 4

2 tablespoons olive oil

Rock salt and freshly ground black pepper, to taste

450 g broccoli florets

Dipping Sauce:

2 teaspoons dried rosemary, crushed

3 garlic cloves, minced

⅓ teaspoon dried marjoram, crushed

60 ml sour cream

80 ml mayonnaise

Lightly grease your broccoli with a thin layer of olive oil. Season with salt and ground black pepper.

Arrange the seasoned broccoli in the air fryer basket. Bake at 202ºC for 15 minutes, shaking once or twice.

In the meantime, prepare the dipping sauce by mixing all the sauce ingredients.

Serve warm broccoli with the dipping sauce and enjoy!

Chapter 6 Snacks and Appetizers

Chapter 6 Snacks and Appetizers

Garlic Edamame

Prep time: 5 minutes | Cook time: 10 minutes | Serves 4

Olive oil
1 (454 g) bag frozen edamame in pods
½ teaspoon salt
½ teaspoon garlic salt

¼ teaspoon freshly ground black pepper
½ teaspoon red pepper flakes (optional)

Spray the air fryer basket lightly with olive oil.
In a medium bowl, add the frozen edamame and lightly spray with olive oil. Toss to coat.
In a small bowl, mix together the salt, garlic salt, black pepper, and red pepper flakes (if using). Add the mixture to the edamame and toss until evenly coated.
Place half the edamame in the air fryer basket. Do not overfill the basket.
Air fry at 192°C for 5 minutes. Shake the basket and cook until the edamame is starting to brown and get crispy, 3 to 5 more minutes. Repeat with the remaining edamame and serve immediately.

Crispy Green Bean Fries with Lemon-Yoghurt Sauce

Prep time: 5 minutes | Cook time: 5 minutes | Serves 4

Green Beans:
1 egg
2 tablespoons water
1 tablespoon wholemeal flour
¼ teaspoon paprika
½ teaspoon garlic powder
½ teaspoon salt
60 ml wholemeal breadcrumbs

227 g whole green beans
Lemon-Yoghurt Sauce:
120 ml non-fat plain Greek yoghurt
1 tablespoon lemon juice
¼ teaspoon salt
⅛ teaspoon cayenne pepper

Make the Green Beans: Preheat the air fryer to 192°C.
In a medium shallow bowl, beat together the egg and water until frothy.
In a separate medium shallow bowl, whisk together the flour, paprika, garlic powder, and salt, then mix in the breadcrumbs.
Spray the bottom of the air fryer with cooking spray.
Dip each green bean into the egg mixture, then into the bread crumb mixture, coating the outside with the crumbs. Place the green beans in a single layer in the bottom of the air fryer basket.
Fry in the air fryer for 5 minutes, or until the breading is golden

brown. Make the Lemon-Yoghurt Sauce:
In a small bowl, combine the yoghurt, lemon juice, salt, and cayenne.
Serve the green bean fries alongside the lemon-yoghurt sauce as a snack or appetizer.

Lemony Pear Chips

Prep time: 15 minutes | Cook time: 9 to 13 minutes | Serves 4

2 firm Bosc or Anjou pears, cut crosswise into ⅛-inch-thick slices
1 tablespoon freshly squeezed

lemon juice
½ teaspoon ground cinnamon
⅛ teaspoon ground cardamom

Preheat the air fryer to 192°C.
Separate the smaller stem-end pear rounds from the larger rounds with seeds. Remove the core and seeds from the larger slices. Sprinkle all slices with lemon juice, cinnamon, and cardamom.
Put the smaller chips into the air fryer basket. Air fry for 3 to 5 minutes, or until light golden brown, shaking the basket once during cooking. Remove from the air fryer.
Repeat with the larger slices, air frying for 6 to 8 minutes, or until light golden brown, shaking the basket once during cooking.
Remove the chips from the air fryer. Cool and serve or store in an airtight container at room temperature up for to 2 days.

Crunchy Tex-Mex Tortilla Chips

Prep time: 5 minutes | Cook time: 5 minutes | Serves 4

Olive oil
½ teaspoon salt
½ teaspoon ground cumin
½ teaspoon chilli powder

½ teaspoon paprika
Pinch cayenne pepper
8 (6-inch) corn tortillas, each cut into 6 wedges

Spray fryer basket lightly with olive oil.
In a small bowl, combine the salt, cumin, chilli powder, paprika, and cayenne pepper.
Place the tortilla wedges in the air fryer basket in a single layer. Spray the tortillas lightly with oil and sprinkle with some of the seasoning mixture. You will need to cook the tortillas in batches.
Air fry at 192°C for 2 to 3 minutes. Shake the basket and cook until the chips are light brown and crispy, an additional 2 to 3 minutes. Watch the chips closely so they do not burn.

Skinny Fries

Prep time: 10 minutes | Cook time: 15 minutes per batch | Serves 2

2 to 3 russet or Maris Piper potatoes, peeled and cut into ¼-inch sticks

2 to 3 teaspoons olive or vegetable oil

Salt, to taste

Cut the potatoes into ¼-inch strips. (A mandolin with a julienne blade is really helpful here.) Rinse the potatoes with cold water several times and let them soak in cold water for at least 10 minutes or as long as overnight.

Preheat the air fryer to 192ºC.

Drain and dry the potato sticks really well, using a clean kitchen towel. Toss the fries with the oil in a bowl and then air fry the fries in two batches at 192ºC for 15 minutes, shaking the basket a couple of times while they cook.

Add the first batch of French fries back into the air fryer basket with the finishing batch and let everything warm through for a few minutes. As soon as the fries are done, season them with salt and transfer to a plate or basket. Serve them warm with ketchup or your favourite dip.

Hush Puppies

Prep time: 45 minutes | Cook time: 10 minutes | Serves 12

240 ml self-raising yellow cornmeal

120 ml plain flour

1 teaspoon sugar

1 teaspoon salt

1 teaspoon freshly ground black pepper

1 large egg

80 ml canned creamed corn

240 ml minced onion

2 teaspoons minced jalapeño pepper

2 tablespoons olive oil, divided

Thoroughly combine the cornmeal, flour, sugar, salt, and pepper in a large bowl.

Whisk together the egg and corn in a small bowl. Pour the egg mixture into the bowl of cornmeal mixture and stir to combine. Stir in the minced onion and jalapeño. Cover the bowl with plastic wrap and place in the refrigerator for 30 minutes.

Preheat the air fryer to 192ºC. Line the air fryer basket with parchment paper and lightly brush it with 1 tablespoon of olive oil.

Scoop out the cornmeal mixture and form into 24 balls, about 1 inch.

Arrange the balls in the parchment paper-lined basket, leaving space between each ball.

Air fry in batches for 5 minutes. Shake the basket and brush the balls with the remaining 1 tablespoon of olive oil. Continue cooking for 5 minutes until golden brown.

Remove the balls (hush puppies) from the basket and serve on a plate.

Pepperoni Pizza Dip

Prep time: 10 minutes | Cook time: 10 minutes | Serves 6

170 g soft white cheese

177 ml shredded Italian cheese blend

60 ml sour cream

1½ teaspoons dried Italian seasoning

¼ teaspoon garlic salt

¼ teaspoon onion powder

177 ml pizza sauce

120 ml sliced miniature pepperoni

60 ml sliced black olives

1 tablespoon thinly sliced green onion

Cut-up raw vegetables, toasted baguette slices, pitta chips, or tortilla chips, for serving

In a small bowl, combine the soft white cheese, 60 ml of the shredded cheese, the sour cream, Italian seasoning, garlic salt, and onion powder. Stir until smooth and the ingredients are well blended.

Spread the mixture in a baking pan. Top with the pizza sauce, spreading to the edges. Sprinkle with the remaining 120 ml shredded cheese. Arrange the pepperoni slices on top of the cheese. Top with the black olives and green onion.

Place the pan in the air fryer basket. Set the air fryer to 176ºC for 10 minutes, or until the pepperoni is beginning to brown on the edges and the cheese is bubbly and lightly browned.

Let stand for 5 minutes before serving with vegetables, toasted baguette slices, pitta chips, or tortilla chips.

Browned Ricotta with Capers and Lemon

Prep time: 10 minutes | Cook time: 8 to 10 minutes | Serves 4 to 6

355 ml whole milk ricotta cheese

2 tablespoons extra-virgin olive oil

2 tablespoons capers, rinsed

Zest of 1 lemon, plus more for garnish

1 teaspoon finely chopped fresh rosemary

Pinch crushed red pepper flakes

Salt and freshly ground black pepper, to taste

1 tablespoon grated Parmesan cheese

Preheat the air fryer to 192ºC.

In a mixing bowl, stir together the ricotta cheese, olive oil, capers, lemon zest, rosemary, red pepper flakes, salt, and pepper until well combined.

Spread the mixture evenly in a baking dish and place it in the air fryer basket.

Air fry for 8 to 10 minutes until the top is nicely browned.

Remove from the basket and top with a sprinkle of grated Parmesan cheese.

Garnish with the lemon zest and serve warm.

Roasted Grape Dip

Prep time: 10 minutes | Cook time: 8 to 12 minutes | Serves 6

475 ml seedless red grapes, rinsed and patted dry
1 tablespoon apple cider vinegar
1 tablespoon honey
240 ml low-fat Greek yoghurt
2 tablespoons semi-skimmed milk
2 tablespoons minced fresh basil

In the air fryer basket, sprinkle the grapes with the cider vinegar and drizzle with the honey. Toss to coat. Roast the grapes at 192ºC for 8 to 12 minutes, or until shrivelled but still soft. Remove from the air fryer.
In a medium bowl, stir together the yoghurt and milk.
Gently blend in the grapes and basil. Serve immediately or cover and chill for 1 to 2 hours.

Crispy Breaded Beef Cubes

Prep time: 10 minutes | Cook time: 12 to 16 minutes | Serves 4

450 g sirloin tip, cut into 1-inch cubes
240 ml cheese pasta sauce
355 ml soft breadcrumbs
2 tablespoons olive oil
½ teaspoon dried marjoram

Preheat the air fryer to 182ºC.
In a medium bowl, toss the beef with the pasta sauce to coat.
In a shallow bowl, combine the breadcrumbs, oil, and marjoram, and mix well. Drop the beef cubes, one at a time, into the bread crumb mixture to coat thoroughly.
Air fry the beef in two batches for 6 to 8 minutes, shaking the basket once during cooking time, until the beef is at least 63ºC and the outside is crisp and brown.
Serve hot.

Homemade Sweet Potato Chips

Prep time: 5 minutes | Cook time: 15 minutes | Serves 2

1 large sweet potato, sliced thin
⅛ teaspoon salt
2 tablespoons olive oil

Preheat the air fryer to 192ºC.
In a small bowl, toss the sweet potatoes, salt, and olive oil together until the potatoes are well coated.
Put the sweet potato slices into the air fryer and spread them out in a single layer.
Fry for 10 minutes. Stir, then air fry for 3 to 5 minutes more, or until the chips reach the preferred level of crispiness.

Cheesy Hash Brown Bruschetta

Prep time: 5 minutes | Cook time: 6 to 8 minutes | Serves 4

4 frozen hash brown patties
1 tablespoon olive oil
80 ml chopped cherry tomatoes
3 tablespoons diced fresh Mozzarella
2 tablespoons grated Parmesan cheese
1 tablespoon balsamic vinegar
1 tablespoon minced fresh basil

4 frozen hash brown patties 1 tablespoon olive oil 80 ml chopped cherry tomatoes 3 tablespoons diced fresh Mozzarella 2 tablespoons grated Parmesan cheese 1 tablespoon balsamic vinegar 1 tablespoon minced fresh basil

Kale Chips with Sesame

Prep time: 15 minutes | Cook time: 8 minutes | Serves 5

2 L deribbed kale leaves, torn into 2-inch pieces
1½ tablespoons olive oil
¾ teaspoon chilli powder
¼ teaspoon garlic powder
½ teaspoon paprika
2 teaspoons sesame seeds

Preheat air fryer to 176ºC.
In a large bowl, toss the kale with the olive oil, chilli powder, garlic powder, paprika, and sesame seeds until well coated.
Put the kale in the air fryer basket and air fry for 8 minutes, flipping the kale twice during cooking, or until the kale is crispy.
Serve warm.

Bacon-Wrapped Shrimp and Jalapeño

Prep time: 20 minutes | Cook time: 26 minutes | Serves 8

24 large shrimp, peeled and deveined, about 340 g
5 tablespoons barbecue sauce,
divided
12 strips bacon, cut in half
24 small pickled jalapeño slices

Toss together the shrimp and 3 tablespoons of the barbecue sauce. Let stand for 15 minutes. Soak 24 wooden toothpicks in water for 10 minutes. Wrap 1 piece bacon around the shrimp and jalapeño slice, then secure with a toothpick.
Preheat the air fryer to 176ºC.
Working in batches, place half of the shrimp in the air fryer basket, spacing them ½ inch apart. Air fry for 10 minutes. Turn shrimp over with tongs and air fry for 3 minutes more, or until bacon is golden brown and shrimp are cooked through.
Brush with the remaining barbecue sauce and serve.

Grilled Ham and Cheese on Raisin Bread

Prep time: 5 minutes | Cook time: 10 minutes | Serves 1

2 slices raisin bread or fruit loaf
2 tablespoons butter, softened
2 teaspoons honey mustard
3 slices thinly sliced honey roast

ham (about 85 g)
4 slices Muenster cheese (about 85 g)
2 toothpicks

Preheat the air fryer to 188°C.

Spread the softened butter on one side of both slices of bread and place the bread, buttered side down on the counter. Spread the honey mustard on the other side of each slice of bread. Layer 2 slices of cheese, the ham and the remaining 2 slices of cheese on one slice of bread and top with the other slice of bread. Remember to leave the buttered side of the bread on the outside.

Transfer the sandwich to the air fryer basket and secure the sandwich with toothpicks.

Air fry for 5 minutes. Flip the sandwich over, remove the toothpicks and air fry for another 5 minutes. Cut the sandwich in half and enjoy!

Mexican Potato Skins

Prep time: 10 minutes | Cook time: 55 minutes | Serves 6

Olive oil
6 medium russet or Maris Piper potatoes, scrubbed
Salt and freshly ground black pepper, to taste
240 ml fat-free refried black

beans
1 tablespoon taco seasoning
120 ml salsa
177 ml low-fat shredded Cheddar cheese

Spray the air fryer basket lightly with olive oil.

Spray the potatoes lightly with oil and season with salt and pepper. Pierce each potato a few times with a fork.

Place the potatoes in the air fryer basket. Air fry at 204°C until fork-tender, 30 to 40 minutes. The cooking time will depend on the size of the potatoes. You can cook the potatoes in the microwave or a standard oven, but they won't get the same lovely crispy skin they will get in the air fryer.

While the potatoes are cooking, in a small bowl, mix together the beans and taco seasoning. Set aside until the potatoes are cool enough to handle.

Cut each potato in half lengthwise. Scoop out most of the insides, leaving about ¼ inch in the skins so the potato skins hold their shape.

Season the insides of the potato skins with salt and black pepper. Lightly spray the insides of the potato skins with oil. You may need to cook them in batches.

Place them into the air fryer basket, skin-side down, and air fry until crisp and golden, 8 to 10 minutes.

Transfer the skins to a work surface and spoon ½ tablespoon of seasoned refried black beans into each one. Top each with 2 teaspoons salsa and 1 tablespoon shredded Cheddar cheese.

Place filled potato skins in the air fryer basket in a single layer. Lightly spray with oil.

Air fry until the cheese is melted and bubbly, 2 to 3 minutes.

Spinach and Crab Meat Cups

Prep time: 10 minutes | Cook time: 10 minutes | Makes 30 cups

1 (170 g) can crab meat, drained to yield 80 ml meat
60 ml frozen spinach, thawed, drained, and chopped
1 clove garlic, minced
120 ml grated Parmesan cheese
3 tablespoons plain yoghurt

¼ teaspoon lemon juice
½ teaspoon Worcestershire sauce
30 mini frozen filo shells, thawed
Cooking spray

Preheat the air fryer to 200°C.

Remove any bits of shell that might remain in the crab meat.

Mix the crab meat, spinach, garlic, and cheese together.

Stir in the yoghurt, lemon juice, and Worcestershire sauce and mix well.

Spoon a teaspoon of filling into each filo shell.

Spray the air fryer basket with cooking spray and arrange half the shells in the basket. Air fry for 5 minutes. Repeat with the remaining shells.

Serve immediately.

Mozzarella Arancini

Prep time: 5 minutes | Cook time: 8 to 11 minutes | Makes 16 arancini

475 ml cooked rice, cooled
2 eggs, beaten
355 ml panko breadcrumbs, divided
120 ml grated Parmesan cheese

2 tablespoons minced fresh basil
16 ¾-inch cubes Mozzarella cheese
2 tablespoons olive oil

Preheat the air fryer to 204°C.

In a medium bowl, combine the rice, eggs, 120 ml of the breadcrumbs, Parmesan cheese, and basil. Form this mixture into 16 1½-inch balls.

Poke a hole in each of the balls with your finger and insert a Mozzarella cube. Form the rice mixture firmly around the cheese.

On a shallow plate, combine the remaining 240 ml of the breadcrumbs with the olive oil and mix well. Roll the rice balls in the breadcrumbs to coat.

Air fry the arancini in batches for 8 to 11 minutes or until golden brown.

Serve hot.

Greek Potato Skins with Olives and Feta

Prep time: 5 minutes | Cook time: 45 minutes | Serves 4

2 russet or Maris Piper potatoes
3 tablespoons olive oil, divided, plus more for drizzling (optional)
1 teaspoon rock salt, divided
¼ teaspoon black pepper

2 tablespoons fresh coriander, chopped, plus more for serving
60 ml Kalamata olives, diced
60 ml crumbled feta
Chopped fresh parsley, for garnish (optional)

Preheat the air fryer to 192ºC.

Using a fork, poke 2 to 3 holes in the potatoes, then coat each with about ½ tablespoon olive oil and ½ teaspoon salt.

Place the potatoes into the air fryer basket and bake for 30 minutes. Remove the potatoes from the air fryer, and slice in half. Using a spoon, scoop out the flesh of the potatoes, leaving a ½-inch layer of potato inside the skins, and set the skins aside.

In a medium bowl, combine the scooped potato middles with the remaining 2 tablespoons of olive oil, ½ teaspoon of salt, black pepper, and coriander. Mix until well combined.

Divide the potato filling into the now-empty potato skins, spreading it evenly over them. Top each potato with a tablespoon each of the olives and feta.

Place the loaded potato skins back into the air fryer and bake for 15 minutes.

Serve with additional chopped coriander or parsley and a drizzle of olive oil, if desired.

Lebanese Muhammara

Prep time: 15 minutes | Cook time: 15 minutes | Serves 6

2 large red peppers
60 ml plus 2 tablespoons extra-virgin olive oil
240 ml walnut halves
1 tablespoon agave nectar or honey
1 teaspoon fresh lemon juice

1 teaspoon ground cumin
1 teaspoon rock salt
1 teaspoon red pepper flakes
Raw vegetables (such as cucumber, carrots, courgette slices, or cauliflower) or toasted pitta chips, for serving

Drizzle the peppers with 2 tablespoons of the olive oil and place in the air fryer basket. Set the air fryer to 204ºC for 10 minutes.

Add the walnuts to the basket, arranging them around the peppers. Set the air fryer to 204ºC for 5 minutes.

Remove the peppers, seal in a resealable plastic bag, and let rest for 5 to 10 minutes. Transfer the walnuts to a plate and set aside to cool.

Place the softened peppers, walnuts, agave, lemon juice, cumin, salt, and ½ teaspoon of the pepper flakes in a food processor and purée until smooth.

Transfer the dip to a serving bowl and make an indentation in the middle. Pour the remaining 60 ml olive oil into the indentation. Garnish the dip with the remaining ½ teaspoon pepper flakes. Serve with vegetables or toasted pitta chips.

Cheesy Steak Fries

Prep time: 5 minutes | Cook time: 20 minutes | Serves 5

1 (794 g) bag frozen steak fries
Cooking spray
Salt and pepper, to taste
120 ml beef gravy

240 ml shredded Mozzarella cheese
2 spring onions, green parts only, chopped

Preheat the air fryer to 204ºC.

Place the frozen steak fries in the air fryer. Air fry for 10 minutes. Shake the basket and spritz the fries with cooking spray. Sprinkle with salt and pepper. Air fry for an additional 8 minutes.

Pour the beef gravy into a medium, microwave-safe bowl. Microwave for 30 seconds, or until the gravy is warm.

Sprinkle the fries with the cheese. Air fry for an additional 2 minutes, until the cheese is melted.

Transfer the fries to a serving dish. Drizzle the fries with gravy and sprinkle the spring onions on top for a green garnish. Serve.

Greek Yoghurt Devilled Eggs

Prep time: 15 minutes | Cook time: 15 minutes | Serves 4

4 eggs
60 ml non-fat plain Greek yoghurt
1 teaspoon chopped fresh dill
⅛ teaspoon salt

⅛ teaspoon paprika
⅛ teaspoon garlic powder
Chopped fresh parsley, for garnish

Preheat the air fryer to 127ºC.

Place the eggs in a single layer in the air fryer basket and cook for 15 minutes.

Quickly remove the eggs from the air fryer and place them into a cold water bath. Let the eggs cool in the water for 10 minutes before removing and peeling them.

After peeling the eggs, cut them in half.

Spoon the yolk into a small bowl. Add the yoghurt, dill, salt, paprika, and garlic powder and mix until smooth.

Spoon or pipe the yolk mixture into the halved egg whites. Serve with a sprinkle of fresh parsley on top.

Veggie Salmon Nachos

Prep time: 10 minutes | Cook time: 9 to 12 minutes | Serves 6

57 g baked no-salt corn tortilla chips

1 (142 g) baked salmon fillet, flaked

120 ml canned low-salt black beans, rinsed and drained

1 red pepper, chopped

120 ml grated carrot

1 jalapeño pepper, minced

80 ml shredded low-salt low-fat Swiss cheese

1 tomato, chopped

Preheat the air fryer to 182°C.

In a baking pan, layer the tortilla chips. Top with the salmon, black beans, red pepper, carrot, jalapeño, and Swiss cheese.

Bake in the air fryer for 9 to 12 minutes, or until the cheese is melted and starts to brown.

Top with the tomato and serve.

Poutine with Waffle Fries

Prep time: 10 minutes | Cook time: 15 to 17 minutes | Serves 4

475 ml frozen waffle cut fries

2 teaspoons olive oil

1 red pepper, chopped

2 spring onions, sliced

240 ml shredded Swiss cheese

120 ml bottled chicken gravy

Preheat the air fryer to 192°C.

Toss the waffle fries with the olive oil and place in the air fryer basket. Air fry for 10 to 12 minutes, or until the fries are crisp and light golden brown, shaking the basket halfway through the cooking time.

Transfer the fries to a baking pan and top with the pepper, spring onions, and cheese. Air fry for 3 minutes, or until the vegetables are crisp and tender.

Remove the pan from the air fryer and drizzle the gravy over the fries. Air fry for 2 minutes, or until the gravy is hot.

Serve immediately.

Ranch Oyster Snack Crackers

Prep time: 3 minutes | Cook time: 12 minutes | Serves 6

Oil, for spraying

60 ml olive oil

2 teaspoons dry ranch seasoning

1 teaspoon chilli powder

½ teaspoon dried dill

½ teaspoon granulated garlic

½ teaspoon salt

1 (255 g) bag oyster crackers or low-salt crackers

Preheat the air fryer to 164°C. Line the air fryer basket with parchment and spray lightly with oil.

In a large bowl, mix together the olive oil, ranch seasoning, chilli powder, dill, garlic, and salt. Add the crackers and toss until evenly coated.

Place the mixture in the prepared basket.

Cook for 10 to 12 minutes, shaking or stirring every 3 to 4 minutes, or until crisp and golden brown.

Veggie Shrimp Toast

Prep time: 15 minutes | Cook time: 3 to 6 minutes | Serves 4

8 large raw shrimp, peeled and finely chopped

1 egg white

2 garlic cloves, minced

3 tablespoons minced red pepper

1 medium celery stalk, minced

2 tablespoons cornflour

¼ teaspoon Chinese five-spice powder

3 slices firm thin-sliced no-salt wholemeal bread

Preheat the air fryer to 176°C.

In a small bowl, stir together the shrimp, egg white, garlic, red pepper, celery, cornflour, and five-spice powder. Top each slice of bread with one-third of the shrimp mixture, spreading it evenly to the edges. With a sharp knife, cut each slice of bread into 4 strips.

Place the shrimp toasts in the air fryer basket in a single layer. You may need to cook them in batches. Air fry for 3 to 6 minutes, until crisp and golden brown.

Serve hot.

Beef and Mango Skewers

Prep time: 10 minutes | Cook time: 4 to 7 minutes | Serves 4

340 g beef sirloin tip, cut into 1-inch cubes

2 tablespoons balsamic vinegar

1 tablespoon olive oil

1 tablespoon honey

½ teaspoon dried marjoram

Pinch of salt

Freshly ground black pepper, to taste

1 mango

Preheat the air fryer to 200°C.

Put the beef cubes in a medium bowl and add the balsamic vinegar, olive oil, honey, marjoram, salt, and pepper. Mix well, then massage the marinade into the beef with your hands. Set aside.

To prepare the mango, stand it on end and cut the skin off, using a sharp knife. Then carefully cut around the oval pit to remove the flesh. Cut the mango into 1-inch cubes.

Thread metal skewers alternating with three beef cubes and two mango cubes.

Roast the skewers in the air fryer basket for 4 to 7 minutes, or until the beef is browned and at least 63°C.

Serve hot.

Spiced Roasted Cashews

Prep time: 5 minutes | Cook time: 10 minutes | Serves 4

475 ml raw cashews
2 tablespoons olive oil
¼ teaspoon salt

¼ teaspoon chilli powder
⅛ teaspoon garlic powder
⅛ teaspoon smoked paprika

Preheat the air fryer to 182°C.

In a large bowl, toss all of the ingredients together.

Pour the cashews into the air fryer basket and roast them for 5 minutes. Shake the basket, then cook for 5 minutes more.

Serve immediately.

Garlicky and Cheesy French Fries

Prep time: 5 minutes | Cook time: 20 to 25 minutes | Serves 4

3 medium russet or Maris Piper potatoes, rinsed, dried, and cut into thin wedges or classic fry shapes
2 tablespoons extra-virgin olive oil
1 tablespoon granulated garlic

80 ml grated Parmesan cheese
½ teaspoon salt
¼ teaspoon freshly ground black pepper
Cooking oil spray
2 tablespoons finely chopped fresh parsley (optional)

In a large bowl combine the potato wedges or fries and the olive oil. Toss to coat.

Sprinkle the potatoes with the granulated garlic, Parmesan cheese, salt, and pepper, and toss again.

Insert the crisper plate into the basket and the basket into the unit. Preheat the unit by selecting AIR FRY, setting the temperature to 204°C, and setting the time to 3 minutes. Select START/STOP to begin.

Once the unit is preheated, spray the crisper plate with cooking oil. Place the potatoes into the basket.

Select AIR FRY, set the temperature to 204°C, and set the time to 20 to 25 minutes. Select START/STOP to begin.

After about 10 minutes, remove the basket and shake it so the fries at the bottom come up to the top. Reinsert the basket to resume cooking.

When the cooking is complete, top the fries with the parsley (if using) and serve hot.

Classic Spring Rolls

Prep time: 10 minutes | Cook time: 9 minutes | Makes 16 spring rolls

4 teaspoons toasted sesame oil
6 medium garlic cloves, minced or pressed
1 tablespoon grated peeled fresh ginger
475 ml thinly sliced shiitake mushrooms
1 L chopped green cabbage

240 ml grated carrot
½ teaspoon sea salt
16 rice paper wrappers
Cooking oil spray (sunflower, safflower, or refined coconut)
Gluten-free sweet and sour sauce or Thai sweet chilli sauce, for serving (optional)

Place a wok or sauté pan over medium heat until hot.

Add the sesame oil, garlic, ginger, mushrooms, cabbage, carrot, and salt. Cook for 3 to 4 minutes, stirring often, until the cabbage is lightly wilted. Remove the pan from the heat.

Gently run a rice paper under water. Lay it on a flat non-absorbent surface. Place about 60 ml of the cabbage filling in the middle. Once the wrapper is soft enough to roll, fold the bottom up over the filling, fold in the sides, and roll the wrapper all the way up. (Basically, make a tiny burrito.)

Repeat step 3 to make the remaining spring rolls until you have the number of spring rolls you want to cook right now (and the amount that will fit in the air fryer basket in a single layer without them touching each other). Refrigerate any leftover filling in an airtight container for about 1 week.

Insert the crisper plate into the basket and the basket into the unit. Preheat the unit by selecting AIR FRY, setting the temperature to 200°C, and setting the time to 3 minutes. Select START/STOP to begin.

Once the unit is preheated, spray the crisper plate and the basket with cooking oil. Place the spring rolls into the basket, leaving a little room between them so they don't stick to each other. Spray the top of each spring roll with cooking oil.

Select AIR FRY, set the temperature to 200°C, and set the time to 9 minutes. Select START/STOP to begin.

When the cooking is complete, the egg rolls should be crisp-ish and lightly browned. Serve immediately, plain or with a sauce of choice.

Chapter 7 Poultry

Chapter 7 Poultry

Turkey Meatloaf

Prep time: 10 minutes | Cook time: 50 minutes | Serves 4

230 g sliced mushrooms
1 small onion, coarsely chopped
2 cloves garlic
680 g 85% lean turkey mince
2 eggs, lightly beaten
1 tablespoon tomato paste
25 g almond meal

2 tablespoons almond milk
1 tablespoon dried oregano
1 teaspoon salt
½ teaspoon freshly ground black pepper
1 Roma tomato, thinly sliced

Preheat the air fryer to 180ºC. . Lightly coat a round pan with olive oil and set aside.

In a food processor fitted with a metal blade, combine the mushrooms, onion, and garlic. Pulse until finely chopped. Transfer the vegetables to a large mixing bowl.

Add the turkey, eggs, tomato paste, almond meal, milk, oregano, salt, and black pepper. Mix gently until thoroughly combined. Transfer the mixture to the prepared pan and shape into a loaf. Arrange the tomato slices on top.

Air fry for 50 minutes or until the meatloaf is nicely browned and a thermometer inserted into the thickest part registers 76ºC. Remove from the air fryer and let rest for about 10 minutes before slicing.

Stuffed Chicken Florentine

Prep time: 10 minutes | Cook time: 20 minutes | Serves 4

3 tablespoons pine nuts
40 g frozen spinach, thawed and squeezed dry
75 g ricotta cheese
2 tablespoons grated Parmesan cheese
3 cloves garlic, minced

Salt and freshly ground black pepper, to taste
4 small boneless, skinless chicken breast halves (about 680 g)
8 slices bacon

Place the pine nuts in a small pan and set in the air fryer basket. Set the air fryer to 200ºC and air fry for 2 to 3 minutes until toasted. Remove the pine nuts to a mixing bowl and continue preheating the air fryer.

In a large bowl, combine the spinach, ricotta, Parmesan, and garlic. Season to taste with salt and pepper and stir well until thoroughly combined.

Using a sharp knife, cut into the chicken breasts, slicing them across and opening them up like a book, but be careful not to cut them all the way through. Sprinkle the chicken with salt and pepper. Spoon equal amounts of the spinach mixture into the chicken, then fold the top of the chicken breast back over the top of the stuffing. Wrap each chicken breast with 2 slices of bacon.

Working in batches if necessary, air fry the chicken for 18 to 20 minutes until the bacon is crisp and a thermometer inserted into the thickest part of the chicken registers 76ºC.

Yellow Curry Chicken Thighs with Peanuts

Prep time: 10 minutes | Cook time: 20 minutes | Serves 6

120 ml unsweetened full-fat coconut milk
2 tablespoons yellow curry paste
1 tablespoon minced fresh ginger

1 tablespoon minced garlic
1 teaspoon kosher salt
450 g boneless, skinless chicken thighs, halved crosswise
2 tablespoons chopped peanuts

In a large bowl, stir together the coconut milk, curry paste, ginger, garlic, and salt until well blended. Add the chicken; toss well to coat. Marinate at room temperature for 30 minutes, or cover and refrigerate for up to 24 hours.

Preheat the air fryer to 190ºC.

Place the chicken (along with marinade) in a baking pan. Place the pan in the air fryer basket. Bake for 20 minutes, turning the chicken halfway through the cooking time. Use a meat thermometer to ensure the chicken has reached an internal temperature of 76ºC. Sprinkle the chicken with the chopped peanuts and serve.

Chicken Nuggets

Prep time: 10 minutes | Cook time: 15 minutes | Serves 4

450 g chicken mince thighs
110 g shredded Mozzarella cheese
1 large egg, whisked

½ teaspoon salt
¼ teaspoon dried oregano
¼ teaspoon garlic powder

In a large bowl, combine all ingredients. Form mixture into twenty nugget shapes, about 2 tablespoons each.

Place nuggets into ungreased air fryer basket, working in batches if needed. Adjust the temperature to (190ºC and air fry for 15 minutes, turning nuggets halfway through cooking. Let cool 5 minutes before serving.

Harissa-Rubbed Chicken

Prep time: 30 minutes | Cook time: 21 minutes | Serves 4

Harissa:

120 ml olive oil

6 cloves garlic, minced

2 tablespoons smoked paprika

1 tablespoon ground coriander

1 tablespoon ground cumin

1 teaspoon ground caraway

1 teaspoon kosher salt

½ to 1 teaspoon cayenne pepper

Chickens:

120 g yogurt

2 small chickens, any giblets removed, split in half lengthwise

For the harissa: In a medium microwave-safe bowl, combine the oil, garlic, paprika, coriander, cumin, caraway, salt, and cayenne. Microwave on high for 1 minute, stirring halfway through the cooking time. (You can also heat this on the stovetop until the oil is hot and bubbling. Or, if you must use your air fryer for everything, cook it in the air fryer at 180ºC for 5 to 6 minutes, or until the paste is heated through.)

For the chicken: In a small bowl, combine 1 to 2 tablespoons harissa and the yogurt. Whisk until well combined. Place the chicken halves in a resealable plastic bag and pour the marinade over. Seal the bag and massage until all of the pieces are thoroughly coated. Marinate at room temperature for 30 minutes or in the refrigerator for up to 24 hours.

Arrange the hen halves in a single layer in the air fryer basket. (If you have a smaller air fryer, you may have to cook this in two batches.) Set the air fryer to 200ºC for 20 minutes. Use a meat thermometer to ensure the chickens have reached an internal temperature of 76ºC.

Cranberry Curry Chicken

Prep time: 12 minutes | Cook time: 18 minutes | Serves 4

3 (140 g) low-sodium boneless, skinless chicken breasts, cut into 1½-inch cubes

2 teaspoons olive oil

2 tablespoons cornflour

1 tablespoon curry powder

1 tart apple, chopped

120 ml low-sodium chicken broth

60 g dried cranberries

2 tablespoons freshly squeezed orange juice

Brown rice, cooked (optional)

Preheat the air fryer to 196ºC.

In a medium bowl, mix the chicken and olive oil. Sprinkle with the cornflour and curry powder. Toss to coat. Stir in the apple and transfer to a metal pan. Bake in the air fryer for 8 minutes, stirring once during cooking.

Add the chicken broth, cranberries, and orange juice. Bake for about 10 minutes more, or until the sauce is slightly thickened and the chicken reaches an internal temperature of 76ºC on a meat thermometer. Serve over hot cooked brown rice, if desired.

Herbed Turkey Breast with Simple Dijon Sauce

Prep time: 5 minutes | Cook time: 30 minutes | Serves 4

1 teaspoon chopped fresh sage

1 teaspoon chopped fresh tarragon

1 teaspoon chopped fresh thyme leaves

1 teaspoon chopped fresh rosemary leaves

1½ teaspoons sea salt

1 teaspoon ground black pepper

1 (900 g) turkey breast

3 tablespoons Dijon mustard

3 tablespoons butter, melted

Cooking spray

Preheat the air fryer to 200ºC. Spritz the air fryer basket with cooking spray.

Combine the herbs, salt, and black pepper in a small bowl. Stir to mix well. Set aside.

Combine the Dijon mustard and butter in a separate bowl. Stir to mix well.

Rub the turkey with the herb mixture on a clean work surface, then brush the turkey with Dijon mixture.

Arrange the turkey in the preheated air fryer basket. Air fry for 30 minutes or until an instant-read thermometer inserted in the thickest part of the turkey breast reaches at least 76ºC.

Transfer the cooked turkey breast on a large plate and slice to serve.

Chicken with Lettuce

Prep time: 15 minutes | Cook time: 14 minutes | Serves 4

450 g chicken breast tenders, chopped into bite-size pieces

½ onion, thinly sliced

½ red bell pepper, seeded and thinly sliced

½ green bell pepper, seeded and thinly sliced

1 tablespoon olive oil

1 tablespoon fajita seasoning

1 teaspoon kosher salt

Juice of ½ lime

8 large lettuce leaves

230 g prepared guacamole

Preheat the air fryer to 200ºC.

In a large bowl, combine the chicken, onion, and peppers. Drizzle with the olive oil and toss until thoroughly coated. Add the fajita seasoning and salt and toss again.

Working in batches if necessary, arrange the chicken and vegetables in a single layer in the air fryer basket. Pausing halfway through the cooking time to shake the basket, air fry for 14 minutes, or until the vegetables are tender and a thermometer inserted into the thickest piece of chicken registers 76ºC.

Transfer the mixture to a serving platter and drizzle with the fresh lime juice. Serve with the lettuce leaves and top with the guacamole.

Easy Chicken Fingers

Prep time: 20 minutes | Cook time: 30 minutes | Makes 12 chicken fingers

60 g all-purpose flour
240 g panko breadcrumbs
2 tablespoons rapeseed oil
1 large egg
3 boneless and skinless chicken

breasts, each cut into 4 strips
Kosher salt and freshly ground
black pepper, to taste
Cooking spray

Preheat the air fryer to 180°C. Spritz the air fryer basket with cooking spray.

Pour the flour in a large bowl. Combine the panko and rapeseed oil on a shallow dish. Whisk the egg in a separate bowl.

Rub the chicken strips with salt and ground black pepper on a clean work surface, then dip the chicken in the bowl of flour. Shake the excess off and dunk the chicken strips in the bowl of whisked egg, then roll the strips over the panko to coat well.

Arrange 4 strips in the air fryer basket each time and air fry for 10 minutes or until crunchy and lightly browned. Flip the strips halfway through. Repeat with remaining ingredients.

Serve immediately.

Chicken Rochambeau

Prep time: 15 minutes | Cook time: 20 minutes | Serves 4

1 tablespoon butter
4 chicken tenders, cut in half
crosswise
Salt and pepper, to taste
30 g flour
Oil for misting
4 slices ham, ¼- to ⅜-inches
thick and large enough to cover
an English muffin
2 English muffins, split

Sauce:
2 tablespoons butter
25 g chopped green onions
50 g chopped mushrooms
2 tablespoons flour
240 ml chicken broth
¼ teaspoon garlic powder
1½ teaspoons Worcestershire
sauce

Place 1 tablespoon of butter in a baking pan and air fry at 200°C for 2 minutes to melt.

Sprinkle chicken tenders with salt and pepper to taste, then roll in the flour.

Place chicken in baking pan, turning pieces to coat with melted butter.

Air fry at 200°C for 5 minutes. Turn chicken pieces over, and spray tops lightly with olive oil. Cook 5 minutes longer or until juices run clear. The chicken will not brown.

While chicken is cooking, make the sauce: In a medium saucepan, melt the 2 tablespoons of butter.

Add onions and mushrooms and sauté until tender, about 3 minutes.

Stir in the flour. Gradually add broth, stirring constantly until you have a smooth gravy.

Add garlic powder and Worcestershire sauce and simmer on low heat until sauce thickens, about 5 minutes.

When chicken is cooked, remove baking pan from air fryer and set aside.

Place ham slices directly into air fryer basket and air fry at 200°C for 5 minutes or until hot and beginning to sizzle a little. Remove and set aside on top of the chicken for now. 1Place the English muffin halves in air fryer basket and air fry at 200°C for 1 minute. 12. Open air fryer and place a ham slice on top of each English muffin half. Stack 2 pieces of chicken on top of each ham slice. Air fry for 1 to 2 minutes to heat through. 13. Place each English muffin stack on a serving plate and top with plenty of sauce.

Pecan-Crusted Chicken Tenders

Prep time: 10 minutes | Cook time: 12 minutes | Serves 4

2 tablespoons mayonnaise
1 teaspoon Dijon mustard
455 g boneless, skinless chicken
tenders

½ teaspoon salt
¼ teaspoon ground black pepper
75 g chopped roasted pecans,
finely ground

In a small bowl, whisk mayonnaise and mustard until combined. Brush mixture onto chicken tenders on both sides, then sprinkle tenders with salt and pepper.

Place pecans in a medium bowl and press each tender into pecans to coat each side.

Place tenders into ungreased air fryer basket in a single layer, working in batches if needed. Adjust the temperature to (190°C and roast for 12 minutes, turning tenders halfway through cooking. Tenders will be golden brown and have an internal temperature of at least 76°C when done. Serve warm.

Cracked-Pepper Chicken Wings

Prep time: 15 minutes | Cook time: 20 minutes | Serves 4

450 g chicken wings
3 tablespoons vegetable oil
60 g all-purpose flour
½ teaspoon smoked paprika

½ teaspoon garlic powder
½ teaspoon kosher salt
1½ teaspoons freshly cracked
black pepper

Place the chicken wings in a large bowl. Drizzle the vegetable oil over wings and toss to coat.

In a separate bowl, whisk together the flour, paprika, garlic powder, salt, and pepper until combined.

Dredge the wings in the flour mixture one at a time, coating them well, and place in the air fryer basket. Set the air fryer to 200°C for 20 minutes, turning the wings halfway through the cooking time, until the breading is browned and crunchy.

Garlic Parmesan Drumsticks

Prep time: 5 minutes | Cook time: 25 minutes | Serves 4

8 (115 g) chicken drumsticks
½ teaspoon salt
⅛ teaspoon ground black pepper
½ teaspoon garlic powder

2 tablespoons salted butter, melted
45 g grated Parmesan cheese
1 tablespoon dried parsley

Sprinkle drumsticks with salt, pepper, and garlic powder. Place drumsticks into ungreased air fryer basket.

Adjust the temperature to 200ºC and air fry for 25 minutes, turning drumsticks halfway through cooking. Drumsticks will be golden and have an internal temperature of at least 76ºC when done.

Transfer drumsticks to a large serving dish. Pour butter over drumsticks, and sprinkle with Parmesan and parsley. Serve warm.

Chicken with Bacon and Tomato

Prep time: 25 minutes | Cook time: 10 minutes | Serves 4

4 medium-sized skin-on chicken drumsticks
1½ teaspoons herbs de Provence
Salt and pepper, to taste
1 tablespoon rice vinegar

2 tablespoons olive oil
2 garlic cloves, crushed
340 g crushed canned tomatoes
1 small-size leek, thinly sliced
2 slices smoked bacon, chopped

Sprinkle the chicken drumsticks with herbs de Provence, salt and pepper; then, drizzle them with rice vinegar and olive oil.

Cook in the baking pan at 180ºC for 8 to 10 minutes. Pause the air fryer; stir in the remaining ingredients and continue to cook for 15 minutes longer; make sure to check them periodically. Bon appétit!

Almond-Crusted Chicken

Prep time: 15 minutes | Cook time: 25 minutes | Serves 4

20 g slivered almonds
2 (170 g) boneless, skinless chicken breasts

2 tablespoons full-fat mayonnaise
1 tablespoon Dijon mustard

Pulse the almonds in a food processor or chop until finely chopped. Place almonds evenly on a plate and set aside.

Completely slice each chicken breast in half lengthwise.

Mix the mayonnaise and mustard in a small bowl and then coat chicken with the mixture.

Lay each piece of chicken in the chopped almonds to fully coat. Carefully move the pieces into the air fryer basket.

Adjust the temperature to 180ºC and air fry for 25 minutes.

Chicken will be done when it has reached an internal temperature of 76ºC or more. Serve warm.

Easy Cajun Chicken Drumsticks

Prep time: 5 minutes | Cook time: 40 minutes | Serves 5

1 tablespoon olive oil
10 chicken drumsticks
1½ tablespoons Cajun seasoning

Salt and ground black pepper, to taste

Preheat the air fryer to 200ºC. Grease the air fryer basket with olive oil.

On a clean work surface, rub the chicken drumsticks with Cajun seasoning, salt, and ground black pepper.

Arrange the seasoned chicken drumsticks in a single layer in the air fryer. You need to work in batches to avoid overcrowding.

Air fry for 18 minutes or until lightly browned. Flip the drumsticks halfway through.

Remove the chicken drumsticks from the air fryer. Serve immediately.

Bacon-Wrapped Chicken Breasts Rolls

Prep time: 10 minutes | Cook time: 15 minutes | Serves 4

15 g chopped fresh chives
2 tablespoons lemon juice
1 teaspoon dried sage
1 teaspoon fresh rosemary leaves
15 g fresh parsley leaves
4 cloves garlic, peeled
1 teaspoon ground fennel
3 teaspoons sea salt

½ teaspoon red pepper flakes
4 (115 g) boneless, skinless chicken breasts, pounded to ¼ inch thick
8 slices bacon
Sprigs of fresh rosemary, for garnish
Cooking spray

Preheat the air fryer to 170ºC. Spritz the air fryer basket with cooking spray.

Put the chives, lemon juice, sage, rosemary, parsley, garlic, fennel, salt, and red pepper flakes in a food processor, then pulse to purée until smooth.

Unfold the chicken breasts on a clean work surface, then brush the top side of the chicken breasts with the sauce.

Roll the chicken breasts up from the shorter side, then wrap each chicken rolls with 2 bacon slices to cover. Secure with toothpicks.

Arrange the rolls in the preheated air fryer, then cook for 10 minutes. Flip the rolls halfway through.

Increase the heat to 200ºC and air fry for 5 more minutes or until the bacon is browned and crispy.

Transfer the rolls to a large plate. Discard the toothpicks and spread with rosemary sprigs before serving.

Chicken Drumsticks with Barbecue-Honey Sauce

Prep time: 5 minutes | Cook time: 40 minutes | Serves 5

1 tablespoon olive oil	Salt and ground black pepper, to
10 chicken drumsticks	taste
Chicken seasoning or rub, to	240 ml barbecue sauce
taste	85 g honey

Preheat the air fryer to 200ºC. Grease the air fryer basket with olive oil.

Rub the chicken drumsticks with chicken seasoning or rub, salt and ground black pepper on a clean work surface.

Arrange the chicken drumsticks in a single layer in the air fryer, then air fry for 18 minutes or until lightly browned. Flip the drumsticks halfway through. You may need to work in batches to avoid overcrowding.

Meanwhile, combine the barbecue sauce and honey in a small bowl. Stir to mix well.

Remove the drumsticks from the air fryer and baste with the sauce mixture to serve.

Spinach and Feta Stuffed Chicken Breasts

Prep time: 10 minutes | Cook time: 27 minutes | Serves 4

1 (280 g) package frozen	pepper
spinach, thawed and drained	4 boneless chicken breasts
well	Salt and freshly ground black
80 g feta cheese, crumbled	pepper, to taste
½ teaspoon freshly ground black	1 tablespoon olive oil

Prepare the filling. Squeeze out as much liquid as possible from the thawed spinach. Rough chop the spinach and transfer it to a mixing bowl with the feta cheese and the freshly ground black pepper.

Prepare the chicken breast. Place the chicken breast on a cutting board and press down on the chicken breast with one hand to keep it stabilized. Make an incision about 1-inch long in the fattest side of the breast. Move the knife up and down inside the chicken breast, without poking through either the top or the bottom, or the other side of the breast. The inside pocket should be about 3-inches long, but the opening should only be about 1-inch wide. If this is too difficult, you can make the incision longer, but you will have to be more careful when cooking the chicken breast since this will expose more of the stuffing.

Once you have prepared the chicken breasts, use your fingers to stuff the filling into each pocket, spreading the mixture down as far as you can.

Preheat the air fryer to 190ºC.

Lightly brush or spray the air fryer basket and the chicken breasts with olive oil. Transfer two of the stuffed chicken breasts to the air fryer. Air fry for 12 minutes, turning the chicken breasts over halfway through the cooking time. Remove the chicken to a resting plate and air fry the second two breasts for 12 minutes. Return the first batch of chicken to the air fryer with the second batch and air fry for 3 more minutes. When the chicken is cooked, an instant read thermometer should register 76ºC in the thickest part of the chicken, as well as in the stuffing.

Remove the chicken breasts and let them rest on a cutting board for 2 to 3 minutes. Slice the chicken on the bias and serve with the slices fanned out.

Bell Pepper Stuffed Chicken Roll-Ups

Prep time: 10 minutes | Cook time: 12 minutes | Serves 4

2 (115 g) boneless, skinless	2 tablespoons taco seasoning
chicken breasts, slice in half	½ green bell pepper, cut into
horizontally	strips
1 tablespoon olive oil	½ red bell pepper, cut into strips
Juice of ½ lime	¼ onion, sliced

Preheat the air fryer to 200ºC.

Unfold the chicken breast slices on a clean work surface. Rub with olive oil, then drizzle with lime juice and sprinkle with taco seasoning.

Top the chicken slices with equal amount of bell peppers and onion. Roll them up and secure with toothpicks.

Arrange the chicken roll-ups in the preheated air fryer. Air fry for 12 minutes or until the internal temperature of the chicken reaches at least 76ºC. Flip the chicken roll-ups halfway through.

Remove the chicken from the air fryer. Discard the toothpicks and serve immediately.

Spice-Rubbed Chicken Thighs

Prep time: 10 minutes | Cook time: 25 minutes | Serves 4

4 (115 g) bone-in, skin-on	2 teaspoons chili powder
chicken thighs	1 teaspoon paprika
½ teaspoon salt	1 teaspoon ground cumin
½ teaspoon garlic powder	1 small lime, halved

Pat chicken thighs dry and sprinkle with salt, garlic powder, chili powder, paprika, and cumin.

Squeeze juice from ½ lime over thighs. Place thighs into ungreased air fryer basket. Adjust the temperature to 190ºC and roast for 25 minutes, turning thighs halfway through cooking. Thighs will be crispy and browned with an internal temperature of at least 76ºC when done.

Transfer thighs to a large serving plate and drizzle with remaining lime juice. Serve warm.

Chipotle Aioli Wings

Prep time: 5 minutes | Cook time: 25 minutes | Serves 6

900 g bone-in chicken wings	2 tablespoons mayonnaise
½ teaspoon salt	2 teaspoons chipotle powder
¼ teaspoon ground black pepper	2 tablespoons lemon juice

In a large bowl, toss wings in salt and pepper, then place into ungreased air fryer basket. Adjust the temperature to 200°C and air fry for 25 minutes, shaking the basket twice while cooking. Wings will be done when golden and have an internal temperature of at least 76°C.

In a small bowl, whisk together mayonnaise, chipotle powder, and lemon juice. Place cooked wings into a large serving bowl and drizzle with aioli. Toss to coat. Serve warm.

Chicken Paillard

Prep time: 10 minutes | Cook time: 10 minutes | Serves 2

2 large eggs, room temperature	Lemon Butter Sauce:
1 tablespoon water	2 tablespoons unsalted butter, melted
40 g powdered Parmesan cheese or pork dust	2 teaspoons lemon juice
2 teaspoons dried thyme leaves	¼ teaspoon finely chopped fresh thyme leaves, plus more for garnish
1 teaspoon ground black pepper	
2 (140 g) boneless, skinless chicken breasts, pounded to ½ inch thick	⅛ teaspoon fine sea salt
	Lemon slices, for serving

Spray the air fryer basket with avocado oil. Preheat the air fryer to 200°C.

Beat the eggs in a shallow dish, then add the water and stir well.

In a separate shallow dish, mix together the Parmesan, thyme, and pepper until well combined.

One at a time, dip the chicken breasts in the eggs and let any excess drip off, then dredge both sides of the chicken in the Parmesan mixture. As you finish, set the coated chicken in the air fryer basket.

Roast the chicken in the air fryer for 5 minutes, then flip the chicken and cook for another 5 minutes, or until cooked through and the internal temperature reaches 76°C.

While the chicken cooks, make the lemon butter sauce: In a small bowl, mix together all the sauce ingredients until well combined.

Plate the chicken and pour the sauce over it. Garnish with chopped fresh thyme and serve with lemon slices.

Store leftovers in an airtight container in the refrigerator for up to 4 days. Reheat in a preheated 200°C air fryer for 5 minutes, or until heated through.

Crunchy Chicken Tenders

Prep time: 5 minutes | Cook time: 12 minutes | Serves 4

1 egg	½ teaspoon dried thyme
60 ml unsweetened almond milk	½ teaspoon dried sage
30 g whole wheat flour	½ teaspoon garlic powder
30 g whole wheat bread crumbs	450 g chicken tenderloins
½ teaspoon salt	1 lemon, quartered
½ teaspoon black pepper	

Preheat the air fryer to 184°C.

In a shallow bowl, beat together the egg and almond milk until frothy.

In a separate shallow bowl, whisk together the flour, bread crumbs, salt, pepper, thyme, sage, and garlic powder.

Dip each chicken tenderloin into the egg mixture, then into the bread crumb mixture, coating the outside with the crumbs. Place the breaded chicken tenderloins into the bottom of the air fryer basket in an even layer, making sure that they don't touch each other.

Cook for 6 minutes, then turn and cook for an additional 5 to 6 minutes. Serve with lemon slices.

Air Fried Chicken Wings with Buffalo Sauce

Prep time: 10 minutes | Cook time: 20 minutes | Serves 6

16 chicken drumettes (party wings)	1 teaspoon garlic powder
	Ground black pepper, to taste
Chicken seasoning or rub, to taste	60 ml buffalo wings sauce
	Cooking spray

Preheat the air fryer to 200°C. Spritz the air fryer basket with cooking spray.

Rub the chicken wings with chicken seasoning, garlic powder, and ground black pepper on a clean work surface.

Arrange the chicken wings in the preheated air fryer. Spritz with cooking spray. Air fry for 10 minutes or until lightly browned. Shake the basket halfway through.

Transfer the chicken wings in a large bowl, then pour in the buffalo wings sauce and toss to coat well.

Put the wings back to the air fryer and cook for an additional 7 minutes.

Serve immediately.

Chapter 8 Beef, Pork, and Lamb

Chapter 8 Beef, Pork, and Lamb

Marinated Steak Tips with Mushrooms

Prep time: 30 minutes | Cook time: 10 minutes | Serves 4

680 g rump steak, trimmed and cut into 1-inch pieces
230 g brown mushrooms, halved
60 ml Worcestershire sauce
1 tablespoon Dijon mustard

1 tablespoon olive oil
1 teaspoon paprika
1 teaspoon crushed red pepper flakes
2 tablespoons chopped fresh parsley (optional)

Place the beef and mushrooms in a gallon-size resealable bag. In a small bowl, whisk together the Worcestershire, mustard, olive oil, paprika, and red pepper flakes. Pour the marinade into the bag and massage gently to ensure the beef and mushrooms are evenly coated. Seal the bag and refrigerate for at least 4 hours, preferably overnight. Remove from the refrigerator 30 minutes before cooking.
Preheat the air fryer to 204ºC.
Drain and discard the marinade. Arrange the steak and mushrooms in the air fryer basket. Air fry for 10 minutes, pausing halfway through the baking time to shake the basket. Transfer to a serving plate and top with the parsley, if desired.

Greek Lamb Pitta Pockets

Prep time: 15 minutes | Cook time: 6 minutes | Serves 4

Dressing:
235 ml plain yogurt
1 tablespoon lemon juice
1 teaspoon dried dill, crushed
1 teaspoon ground oregano
½ teaspoon salt
Meatballs:
230 g lamb mince
1 tablespoon diced onion
1 teaspoon dried parsley
1 teaspoon dried dill, crushed
¼ teaspoon oregano

¼ teaspoon coriander
¼ teaspoon ground cumin
¼ teaspoon salt
4 pitta halves
Suggested Toppings:
1 red onion, slivered
1 medium cucumber, deseeded, thinly sliced
Crumbled feta cheese
Sliced black olives
Chopped fresh peppers

Preheat the air fryer to 200ºC.
Stir the dressing ingredients together in a small bowl and refrigerate while preparing lamb.
Combine all meatball ingredients in a large bowl and stir to distribute seasonings.

Shape meat mixture into 12 small meatballs, rounded or slightly flattened if you prefer.
Transfer the meatballs in the preheated air fryer and air fry for 6 minutes, until well done. Remove and drain on paper towels.
To serve, pile meatballs and the choice of toppings in pitta pockets and drizzle with dressing.

Herbed Beef

Prep time: 5 minutes | Cook time: 22 minutes | Serves 6

1 teaspoon dried dill
1 teaspoon dried thyme
1 teaspoon garlic powder

900 g beef steak
3 tablespoons butter

Preheat the air fryer to 182ºC.
Combine the dill, thyme, and garlic powder in a small bowl, and massage into the steak.
Air fry the steak in the air fryer for 20 minutes, then remove, shred, and return to the air fryer.
Add the butter and air fry the shredded steak for a further 2 minutes at 185ºC. Make sure the beef is coated in the butter before serving.

Ham Hock Mac and Cheese

Prep time: 20 minutes | Cook time: 25 minutes | Serves 4

2 large eggs, beaten
475 ml cottage cheese, full-fat or low-fat
475 ml grated sharp Cheddar cheese, divided
235 ml sour cream
½ teaspoon salt

1 teaspoon freshly ground black pepper
475 ml uncooked elbow macaroni
2 ham hocks (about 310 g each), meat removed and diced
1 to 2 tablespoons oil

In a large bowl, stir together the eggs, cottage cheese, 235 ml of the Cheddar cheese, sour cream, salt, and pepper.
Stir in the macaroni and the diced meat.
Preheat the air fryer to 182ºC. Spritz a baking pan with oil.
Pour the macaroni mixture into the prepared pan, making sure all noodles are covered with sauce.
Cook for 12 minutes. Stir in the remaining 235 ml of Cheddar cheese, making sure all the noodles are covered with sauce. Cook for 13 minutes more, until the noodles are tender. Let rest for 5 minutes before serving.

Beef Whirls

Prep time: 30 minutes | Cook time: 18 minutes | Serves 6

3 minute steaks (170 g each)
1 (450 g) bottle Italian dressing
235 ml Italian-style bread crumbs (or plain bread crumbs with Italian seasoning to taste)
120 ml grated Parmesan cheese
1 teaspoon dried basil
1 teaspoon dried oregano
1 teaspoon dried parsley
60 ml beef stock
1 to 2 tablespoons oil

In a large resealable bag, combine the steaks and Italian dressing. Seal the bag and refrigerate to marinate for 2 hours.

In a medium bowl, whisk the bread crumbs, cheese, basil, oregano, and parsley until blended. Stir in the beef stock.

Place the steaks on a cutting board and cut each in half so you have 6 equal pieces. Sprinkle with the bread crumb mixture. Roll up the steaks, jelly roll-style, and secure with toothpicks.

Preheat the air fryer to 204°C.

Place 3 roll-ups in the air fryer basket.

Cook for 5 minutes. Flip the roll-ups and spritz with oil. Cook for 4 minutes more until the internal temperature reaches 64°C. Repeat with the remaining roll-ups. Let rest for 5 to 10 minutes before serving.

Ham with Sweet Potatoes

Prep time: 20 minutes | Cook time: 15 to 17 minutes | Serves 4

235 ml freshly squeezed orange juice
120 ml packed light brown sugar
1 tablespoon Dijon mustard
½ teaspoon salt
½ teaspoon freshly ground black
pepper
3 sweet potatoes, cut into small wedges
2 gammon steaks (230 g each), halved
1 to 2 tablespoons oil

In a large bowl, whisk the orange juice, brown sugar, Dijon, salt, and pepper until blended. Toss the sweet potato wedges with the brown sugar mixture.

Preheat the air fryer to 204°C. Line the air fryer basket with parchment paper and spritz with oil.

Place the sweet potato wedges on the parchment.

Cook for 10 minutes.

Place gammon steaks on top of the sweet potatoes and brush everything with more of the orange juice mixture.

Cook for 3 minutes. Flip the gammon and cook or 2 to 4 minutes more until the sweet potatoes are soft and the glaze has thickened.

Cut the gammon steaks in half to serve.

Bean and Beef Meatball Taco Pizza

Prep time: 10 minutes | Cook time: 7 to 9 minutes per batch | Serves 4

180 ml refried beans (from a 450 g can)
120 ml salsa
10 frozen precooked beef meatballs, thawed and sliced
1 jalapeño pepper, sliced
4 whole-wheat pitta breads
235 ml shredded chilli cheese
120 ml shredded Monterey Jack or Cheddar cheese
Cooking oil spray
80 ml sour cream

In a medium bowl, stir together the refried beans, salsa, meatballs, and jalapeño.

Insert the crisper plate into the basket and the basket into the unit. Preheat the unit by selecting BAKE, setting the temperature to 192°C, and setting the time to 3 minutes. Select START/STOP to begin.

Top the pittas with the refried bean mixture and sprinkle with the cheeses.

Once the unit is preheated, spray the crisper plate with cooking oil. Working in batches, place the pizzas into the basket. Select BAKE, set the temperature to 192°C, and set the time to 9 minutes. Select START/STOP to begin.

After about 7 minutes, check the pizzas. They are done when the cheese is melted and starts to brown. If not ready, resume cooking. When the cooking is complete, top each pizza with a dollop of sour cream and serve warm.

Greek Lamb Rack

Prep time: 5 minutes | Cook time: 10 minutes | Serves 4

60 ml freshly squeezed lemon juice
1 teaspoon oregano
2 teaspoons minced fresh rosemary
1 teaspoon minced fresh thyme
2 tablespoons minced garlic
Salt and freshly ground black pepper, to taste
2 to 4 tablespoons olive oil
1 lamb rib rack (7 to 8 ribs)

Preheat the air fryer to 182°C.

In a small mixing bowl, combine the lemon juice, oregano, rosemary, thyme, garlic, salt, pepper, and olive oil and mix well.

Rub the mixture over the lamb, covering all the meat. Put the rack of lamb in the air fryer. Roast for 10 minutes. Flip the rack halfway through.

After 10 minutes, measure the internal temperature of the rack of lamb reaches at least 64°C.

Serve immediately.

Sumptuous Pizza Tortilla Rolls

Prep time: 10 minutes | Cook time: 6 minutes | Serves 4

1 teaspoon butter
½ medium onion, slivered
½ red or green pepper, julienned
110 g fresh white mushrooms, chopped
120 ml pizza sauce

8 flour tortillas
8 thin slices wafer-thinham
24 pepperoni slices
235 ml shredded Mozzarella cheese
Cooking spray

Preheat the air fryer to 200°C.

Put butter, onions, pepper, and mushrooms in a baking pan. Bake in the preheated air fryer for 3 minutes. Stir and cook 3 to 4 minutes longer until just crisp and tender. Remove pan and set aside.

To assemble rolls, spread about 2 teaspoons of pizza sauce on one half of each tortilla. Top with a slice of ham and 3 slices of pepperoni. Divide sautéed vegetables among tortillas and top with cheese.

Roll up tortillas, secure with toothpicks if needed, and spray with oil.

Put 4 rolls in air fryer basket and air fry for 4 minutes. Turn and air fry 4 minutes, until heated through and lightly browned.

Repeat step 4 to air fry remaining pizza rolls.

Serve immediately.

Filipino Crispy Pork Belly

Prep time: 20 minutes | Cook time: 30 minutes | Serves 4

450 g pork belly
700 ml water
6 garlic cloves
2 tablespoons soy sauce

1 teaspoon coarse or flaky salt
1 teaspoon black pepper
2 bay leaves

Cut the pork belly into three thick chunks so it will cook more evenly.

Place the pork, water, garlic, soy sauce, salt, pepper, and bay leaves in the inner pot of an Instant Pot or other electric pressure cooker. Seal and cook at high pressure for 15 minutes. Let the pressure release naturally for 10 minutes, then manually release the remaining pressure. (If you do not have a pressure cooker, place all the ingredients in a large saucepan. Cover and cook over low heat until a knife can be easily inserted into the skin side of pork belly, about 1 hour.) Using tongs, very carefully transfer the meat to a wire rack over a rimmed baking sheet to drain and dry for 10 minutes.

Cut each chunk of pork belly into two long slices. Arrange the slices in the air fryer basket. Set the air fryer to 204°C for 15 minutes, or until the fat has crisped.

Serve immediately.

Pork Milanese

Prep time: 10 minutes | Cook time: 12 minutes | Serves 4

4 (1-inch) boneless pork chops
Fine sea salt and ground black pepper, to taste
2 large eggs
180 ml pre-grated Parmesan

cheese
Chopped fresh parsley, for garnish
Lemon slices, for serving

Spray the air fryer basket with avocado oil. Preheat the air fryer to 204°C.

Place the pork chops between 2 sheets of plastic wrap and pound them with the flat side of a meat tenderizer until they're ¼ inch thick. Lightly season both sides of the chops with salt and pepper.

Lightly beat the eggs in a shallow bowl. Divide the Parmesan cheese evenly between 2 bowls and set the bowls in this order: Parmesan, eggs, Parmesan. Dredge a chop in the first bowl of Parmesan, then dip it in the eggs, and then dredge it again in the second bowl of Parmesan, making sure both sides and all edges are well coated. Repeat with the remaining chops.

Place the chops in the air fryer basket and air fry for 12 minutes, or until the internal temperature reaches 64°C, flipping halfway through.

Garnish with fresh parsley and serve immediately with lemon slices. Store leftovers in an airtight container in the refrigerator for up to 3 days. Reheat in a preheated 200°C air fryer for 5 minutes, or until warmed through.

Sweet and Spicy Country-Style Ribs

Prep time: 10 minutes | Cook time: 25 minutes | Serves 4

2 tablespoons brown sugar
2 tablespoons smoked paprika
1 teaspoon garlic powder
1 teaspoon onion granules
1 teaspoon mustard powder
1 teaspoon ground cumin

1 teaspoon coarse or flaky salt
1 teaspoon black pepper
¼ to ½ teaspoon cayenne pepper
680 g boneless pork steaks
235 ml barbecue sauce

In a small bowl, stir together the brown sugar, paprika, garlic powder, onion granules, mustard powder, cumin, salt, black pepper, and cayenne. Mix until well combined.

Pat the ribs dry with a paper towel. Generously sprinkle the rub evenly over both sides of the ribs and rub in with your fingers.

Place the ribs in the air fryer basket. Set the air fryer to 176°C for 15 minutes. Turn the ribs and brush with 120 ml of the barbecue sauce. Cook for an additional 10 minutes. Use a meat thermometer to ensure the pork has reached an internal temperature of 64°C.

Serve with remaining barbecue sauce.

BBQ Pork Steaks

Prep time: 5 minutes | Cook time: 15 minutes | Serves 4

4 pork steaks

1 tablespoon Cajun seasoning

2 tablespoons BBQ sauce

1 tablespoon vinegar

1 teaspoon soy sauce

120 ml brown sugar

120 ml ketchup

Preheat the air fryer to 143ºC.

Sprinkle pork steaks with Cajun seasoning.

Combine remaining ingredients and brush onto steaks.

Add coated steaks to air fryer. Air fry 15 minutes until just browned.

Serve immediately.

Beef and Pork Sausage Meatloaf

Prep time: 20 minutes | Cook time: 25 minutes | Serves 4

340 g beef mince

110 g pork sausage meat

235 ml shallots, finely chopped

2 eggs, well beaten

3 tablespoons milk

1 tablespoon oyster sauce

1 teaspoon porcini mushrooms

½ teaspoon cumin powder

1 teaspoon garlic paste

1 tablespoon fresh parsley

Salt and crushed red pepper flakes, to taste

235 ml crushed cream crackers

Cooking spray

Preheat the air fryer to 182ºC. Spritz a baking dish with cooking spray.

Mix all the ingredients in a large bowl, combining everything well.

Transfer to the baking dish and bake in the air fryer for 25 minutes.

Serve hot.

Bacon, Cheese and Pear Stuffed Pork

Prep time: 10 minutes | Cook time: 24 minutes | Serves 3

4 slices bacon, chopped

1 tablespoon butter

120 ml finely diced onion

80 ml chicken stock

355 ml seasoned stuffing mix

1 egg, beaten

½ teaspoon dried thyme

½ teaspoon salt

⅛ teaspoon black pepper

1 pear, finely diced

80 ml crumbled blue cheese

3 boneless pork chops (2-inch thick)

Olive oil

Salt and freshly ground black pepper, to taste

Preheat the air fryer to 204ºC.

Place the bacon into the air fryer basket and air fry for 6 minutes, stirring halfway through the cooking time. Remove the bacon and set it aside on a paper towel. Pour out the grease from the bottom of the air fryer.

Make the stuffing: Melt the butter in a medium saucepan over medium heat on the stovetop. Add the onion and sauté for a few minutes, until it starts to soften. Add the chicken stock and simmer for 1 minute. Remove the pan from the heat and add the stuffing mix. Stir until the stock has been absorbed. Add the egg, dried thyme, salt and freshly ground black pepper, and stir until combined. Fold in the diced pear and crumbled blue cheese.

Place the pork chops on a cutting board. Using the palm of your hand to hold the chop flat and steady, slice into the side of the pork chop to make a pocket in the center of the chop. Leave about an inch of chop uncut and make sure you don't cut all the way through the pork chop. Brush both sides of the pork chops with olive oil and season with salt and freshly ground black pepper. Stuff each pork chop with a third of the stuffing, packing the stuffing tightly inside the pocket.

Preheat the air fryer to 182ºC.

Spray or brush the sides of the air fryer basket with oil. Place the pork chops in the air fryer basket with the open stuffed edge of the pork chop facing the outside edges of the basket.

Air fry the pork chops for 18 minutes, turning the pork chops over halfway through the cooking time. When the chops are done, let them rest for 5 minutes and then transfer to a serving platter.

Beef Burgers with Mushroom

Prep time: 10 minutes | Cook time: 21 to 23 minutes | Serves 4

450 g beef mince, formed into 4 patties

Sea salt and freshly ground black pepper, to taste

235 ml thinly sliced onion

230 g mushrooms, sliced

1 tablespoon avocado oil

60 g Gruyère cheese, shredded (about 120 ml)

Season the patties on both sides with salt and pepper.

Set the air fryer to 192ºC. Place the patties in the basket and cook for 3 minutes. Flip and cook for another 2 minutes. Remove the burgers and set aside.

Place the onion and mushrooms in a medium bowl. Add the avocado oil and salt and pepper to taste; toss well.

Place the onion and mushrooms in the air fryer basket. Cook for 15 minutes, stirring occasionally.

Spoon the onions and mushrooms over the patties. Top with the cheese. Place the patties back in the air fryer basket and cook for another 1 to 3 minutes, until the cheese melts and an instant-read thermometer reads 72ºC. Remove and let rest. The temperature will rise to 74ºC, yielding a perfect medium-well burger.

Parmesan-Crusted Pork Chops

Prep time: 5 minutes | Cook time: 12 minutes | Serves 4

1 large egg
120 ml grated Parmesan cheese
4 (110 g) boneless pork chops
½ teaspoon salt
¼ teaspoon ground black pepper

Whisk egg in a medium bowl and place Parmesan in a separate medium bowl.

Sprinkle pork chops on both sides with salt and pepper. Dip each pork chop into egg, then press both sides into Parmesan.

Place pork chops into ungreased air fryer basket. Adjust the temperature to 204°C and air fry for 12 minutes, turning chops halfway through cooking. Pork chops will be golden and have an internal temperature of at least 64°C when done. Serve warm.

Lamb and Cucumber Burgers

Prep time: 8 minutes | Cook time: 15 to 18 minutes | Serves 4

1 teaspoon ground ginger
½ teaspoon ground coriander
¼ teaspoon freshly ground white pepper
½ teaspoon ground cinnamon
½ teaspoon dried oregano
¼ teaspoon ground allspice
¼ teaspoon ground turmeric
120 ml low-fat plain Greek
yogurt
450 g lamb mince
1 teaspoon garlic paste
¼ teaspoon salt
¼ teaspoon freshly ground black pepper
Cooking oil spray
4 hamburger buns
½ cucumber, thinly sliced

In a small bowl, stir together the ginger, coriander, white pepper, cinnamon, oregano, allspice, and turmeric.

Put the yogurt in a small bowl and add half the spice mixture. Mix well and refrigerate.

Insert the crisper plate into the basket and the basket into the unit. Preheat the unit by selecting AIR FRY, setting the temperature to 182°C, and setting the time to 3 minutes. Select START/STOP to begin.

In a large bowl, combine the lamb, garlic paste, remaining spice mix, salt, and pepper. Gently but thoroughly mix the ingredients with your hands. Form the meat into 4 patties.

Once the unit is preheated, spray the crisper plate with cooking oil, and place the patties into the basket.

Select AIR FRY, set the temperature to 182°C, and set the time to 18 minutes. Select START/STOP to begin.

After 15 minutes, check the burgers. If a food thermometer inserted into the burgers registers 72°C, the burgers are done. If not, resume cooking.

When the cooking is complete, assemble the burgers on the buns with cucumber slices and a dollop of the yogurt dip.

Beef Fillet with Thyme and Parsley

Prep time: 5 minutes | Cook time: 15 minutes | Serves 4

1 tablespoon butter, melted
¼ dried thyme
1 teaspoon garlic salt
¼ teaspoon dried parsley
450 g beef fillet

Preheat the air fryer to 204°C.

In a bowl, combine the melted butter, thyme, garlic salt, and parsley.

Cut the beef fillet into slices and generously apply the seasoned butter using a brush. Transfer to the air fryer basket.

Air fry the beef for 15 minutes.

Take care when removing it and serve hot.

Spaghetti Zoodles and Meatballs

Prep time: 30 minutes | Cook time: 11 to 13 minutes | Serves 6

450 g beef mince
1½ teaspoons sea salt, plus more for seasoning
1 large egg, beaten
1 teaspoon gelatin
180 ml Parmesan cheese
2 teaspoons minced garlic
1 teaspoon Italian seasoning
Freshly ground black pepper, to taste
Avocado oil spray
Keto-friendly marinara sauce, for serving
170 g courgette noodles, made using a spiralizer or store-bought

Place the beef mince in a large bowl, and season with the salt.

Place the egg in a separate bowl and sprinkle with the gelatin. Allow to sit for 5 minutes.

Stir the gelatin mixture, then pour it over the ground beef. Add the Parmesan, garlic, and Italian seasoning. Season with salt and pepper.

Form the mixture into 1½-inch meatballs and place them on a plate; cover with plastic wrap and refrigerate for at least 1 hour or overnight.

Spray the meatballs with oil. Set the air fryer to 204°C and arrange the meatballs in a single layer in the air fryer basket. Air fry for 4 minutes. Flip the meatballs and spray them with more oil. Air fry for 4 minutes more, until an instant-read thermometer reads 72°C. Transfer the meatballs to a plate and allow them to rest.

While the meatballs are resting, heat the marinara in a saucepan on the stove over medium heat.

Place the courgette noodles in the air fryer, and cook at 204°C for 3 to 5 minutes.

To serve, place the courgette noodles in serving bowls. Top with meatballs and warm marinara.

Southern Chili

Prep time: 20 minutes | Cook time: 25 minutes | Serves 4

450 g beef mince (85% lean)
235 ml minced onion
1 (794 g) can tomato purée
1 (425 g) can diced tomatoes

1 (425 g) can red kidney beans, rinsed and drained
60 ml Chili seasoning

Preheat the air fryer to 204ºC.

In a baking pan, mix the mince and onion. Place the pan in the air fryer.

Cook for 4 minutes. Stir and cook for 4 minutes more until browned. Remove the pan from the fryer. Drain the meat and transfer to a large bowl.

Reduce the air fryer temperature to 176ºC.

To the bowl with the meat, add in the tomato purée, diced tomatoes, kidney beans, and Chili seasoning. Mix well. Pour the mixture into the baking pan.

Cook for 25 minutes, stirring every 10 minutes, until thickened.

Sausage and Courgette Lasagna

Prep time: 25 minutes | Cook time: 56 minutes | Serves 4

1 courgette
Avocado oil spray
170 g hot Italian-seasoned sausage, casings removed
60 g mushrooms, stemmed and sliced
1 teaspoon minced garlic
235 ml keto-friendly marinara sauce

180 ml ricotta cheese
235 ml shredded gruyere cheese, divided
120 ml finely grated Parmesan cheese
Sea salt and freshly ground black pepper, to taste
Fresh basil, for garnish

Cut the courgette into long thin slices using a mandoline slicer or sharp knife. Spray both sides of the slices with oil.

Place the slices in a single layer in the air fryer basket, working in batches if necessary. Set the air fryer to 164ºC and air fry for 4 to 6 minutes, until most of the moisture has been released from the courgette.

Place a large skillet over medium-high heat. Crumble the sausage into the hot skillet and cook for 6 minutes, breaking apart the meat with the back of a spoon. Remove the sausage from the skillet, leaving any fats that remain. Add the mushrooms to the skillet and cook for 10 minutes, until the liquid nearly evaporates. Add the garlic and cook for 1 minute more. Stir in the marinara and cook for 2 more minutes.

In a medium bowl, combine the ricotta cheese, 120 ml of gruyere cheese, Parmesan cheese, and salt and pepper to taste.

Spread 60 ml of the meat sauce in the bottom of a deep pan (or other pan that fits inside your air fryer). Top with half of the courgette slices. Add half of the cheese mixture. Top the cheese with half of the remaining meat sauce. Layer the remaining courgette over the meat sauce and top with the remaining cheese mixture. Top the lasagna with the remaining 120 ml of fontina cheese.

Cover the lasagna with aluminum foil or parchment paper and place it in the air fryer. Bake for 25 minutes. Remove the foil and cook for 8 to 10 minutes more.

Allow the lasagna to rest for 15 minutes before cutting and serving. Garnish with basil.

Lamb Burger with Feta and Olives

Prep time: 10 minutes | Cook time: 20 minutes | Serves 3 to 4

2 teaspoons olive oil
⅓ onion, finely chopped
1 clove garlic, minced
450 g lamb mince
2 tablespoons fresh parsley, finely chopped
1½ teaspoons fresh oregano, finely chopped

120 ml black olives, finely chopped
80 ml crumbled feta cheese
½ teaspoon salt
Freshly ground black pepper, to taste
4 thick pitta breads

Preheat a medium skillet over medium-high heat on the stovetop. Add the olive oil and cook the onion until tender, but not browned, about 4 to 5 minutes. Add the garlic and cook for another minute. Transfer the onion and garlic to a mixing bowl and add the lamb mince, parsley, oregano, olives, feta cheese, salt and pepper. Gently mix the ingredients together.

Divide the mixture into 3 or 4 equal portions and then form the hamburgers, being careful not to over-handle the meat. One good way to do this is to throw the meat back and forth between your hands like a baseball, packing the meat each time you catch it. Flatten the balls into patties, making an indentation in the center of each patty. Flatten the sides of the patties as well to make it easier to fit them into the air fryer basket.

Preheat the air fryer to 188ºC.

If you don't have room for all four burgers, air fry two or three burgers at a time for 8 minutes at 188ºC. Flip the burgers over and air fry for another 8 minutes. If you cooked your burgers in batches, return the first batch of burgers to the air fryer for the last two minutes of cooking to re-heat. This should give you a medium-well burger. If you'd prefer a medium-rare burger, shorten the cooking time to about 13 minutes. Remove the burgers to a resting plate and let the burgers rest for a few minutes before dressing and serving.

While the burgers are resting, toast the pitta breads in the air fryer for 2 minutes. Tuck the burgers into the toasted pitta breads, or wrap the pittas around the burgers and serve with a tzatziki sauce or some mayonnaise.

Bacon-Wrapped Vegetable Kebabs

Prep time: 10 minutes | Cook time: 10 to 12 minutes | Serves 4

110 g mushrooms, sliced
1 small courgette, sliced
12 baby plum tomatoes
110 g sliced bacon, halved

Avocado oil spray
Sea salt and freshly ground black pepper, to taste

Stack 3 mushroom slices, 1 courgette slice, and 1 tomato. Wrap a bacon strip around the vegetables and thread them onto a skewer. Repeat with the remaining vegetables and bacon. Spray with oil and sprinkle with salt and pepper.

Set the air fryer to 204°C. Place the skewers in the air fryer basket in a single layer, working in batches if necessary, and air fry for 5 minutes. Flip the skewers and cook for 5 to 7 minutes more, until the bacon is crispy and the vegetables are tender.

Serve warm.

Cheesy Low-Carb Lasagna

Prep time: 10 minutes | Cook time: 10 minutes | Serves 4

Meat Layer:
Extra-virgin olive oil
450 g 85% lean beef mince
235 ml marinara sauce
60 ml diced celery
60 ml diced red onion
½ teaspoon minced garlic
Coarse or flaky salt and black pepper, to taste
Cheese Layer:

230 g ricotta cheese
235 ml shredded Mozzarella cheese
120 ml grated Parmesan cheese
2 large eggs
1 teaspoon dried Italian seasoning, crushed
½ teaspoon each minced garlic, garlic powder, and black pepper

For the meat layer: Grease a cake pan with 1 teaspoon olive oil.

In a large bowl, combine the beef mince, marinara, celery, onion, garlic, salt, and pepper. Place the seasoned meat in the pan.

Place the pan in the air fryer basket. Set the air fryer to 192°C for 10 minutes.

Meanwhile, for the cheese layer: In a medium bowl, combine the ricotta, half the Mozzarella, the Parmesan, lightly beaten eggs, Italian seasoning, minced garlic, garlic powder, and pepper. Stir until well blended.

At the end of the cooking time, spread the cheese mixture over the meat mixture. Sprinkle with the remaining 120 ml Mozzarella. Set the air fryer to 192°C for 10 minutes, or until the cheese is browned and bubbling.

At the end of the cooking time, use a meat thermometer to ensure the meat has reached an internal temperature of 72°C.

Drain the fat and liquid from the pan. Let stand for 5 minutes before serving.

Pork Medallions with Endive Salad

Prep time: 25 minutes | Cook time: 7 minutes | Serves 4

1 (230 g) pork tenderloin
Salt and freshly ground black pepper, to taste
60 ml flour
2 eggs, lightly beaten
180 ml finely crushed crackers
1 teaspoon paprika
1 teaspoon mustard powder
1 teaspoon garlic powder
1 teaspoon dried thyme
1 teaspoon salt
vegetable or rapeseed oil, in spray bottle
Vinaigrette:
60 ml white balsamic vinegar
2 tablespoons agave syrup (or

honey or maple syrup)
1 tablespoon Dijon mustard
juice of ½ lemon
2 tablespoons chopped chervil or flat-leaf parsley
salt and freshly ground black pepper
120 ml extra-virgin olive oil
Endive Salad:
1 heart romaine lettuce, torn into large pieces
2 heads endive, sliced
120 ml cherry tomatoes, halved
85 g fresh Mozzarella, diced
Salt and freshly ground black pepper, to taste

Slice the pork tenderloin into 1-inch slices. Using a meat pounder, pound the pork slices into thin ½-inch medallions. Generously season the pork with salt and freshly ground black pepper on both sides.

Set up a dredging station using three shallow dishes. Put the flour in one dish and the beaten eggs in a second dish. Combine the crushed crackers, paprika, mustard powder, garlic powder, thyme and salt in a third dish.

Preheat the air fryer to 204°C.

Dredge the pork medallions in flour first and then into the beaten egg. Let the excess egg drip off and coat both sides of the medallions with the cracker crumb mixture. Spray both sides of the coated medallions with vegetable or rapeseed oil.

Air fry the medallions in two batches at 204°C for 5 minutes. Once you have air-fried all the medallions, flip them all over and return the first batch of medallions back into the air fryer on top of the second batch. Air fry at 204°C for an additional 2 minutes.

While the medallions are cooking, make the salad and dressing. Whisk the white balsamic vinegar, agave syrup, Dijon mustard, lemon juice, chervil, salt and pepper together in a small bowl. Whisk in the olive oil slowly until combined and thickened.

Combine the romaine lettuce, endive, cherry tomatoes, and Mozzarella cheese in a large salad bowl. Drizzle the dressing over the vegetables and toss to combine. Season with salt and freshly ground black pepper.

Serve the pork medallions warm on or beside the salad.

Sesame Beef Lettuce Tacos

Prep time: 30 minutes | Cook time: 8 to 10 minutes | Serves 4

60 ml soy sauce or tamari

60 ml avocado oil

2 tablespoons cooking sherry

1 tablespoon granulated sweetener

1 tablespoon ground cumin

1 teaspoon minced garlic

Sea salt and freshly ground black pepper, to taste

450 g bavette or skirt steak

8 butterhead lettuce leaves

2 spring onions, sliced

1 tablespoon toasted sesame seeds

Hot sauce, for serving

Lime wedges, for serving

Flaky sea salt (optional)

In a small bowl, whisk together the soy sauce, avocado oil, cooking sherry, sweetener, cumin, garlic, and salt and pepper to taste.

Place the steak in a shallow dish. Pour the marinade over the beef. Cover the dish with plastic wrap and let it marinate in the refrigerator for at least 2 hours or overnight.

Remove the flank steak from the dish and discard the marinade.

Set the air fryer to 204ºC. Place the steak in the air fryer basket and air fry for 4 to 6 minutes. Flip the steak and cook for 4 minutes more, until an instant-read thermometer reads 49ºC at the thickest part (or cook it to your desired doneness). Allow the steak to rest for 10 minutes, then slice it thinly against the grain.

Stack 2 lettuce leaves on top of each other and add some sliced meat. Top with spring onions and sesame seeds. Drizzle with hot sauce and lime juice, and finish with a little flaky salt (if using). Repeat with the remaining lettuce leaves and fillings.

Mediterranean Beef Steaks

Prep time: 20 minutes | Cook time: 20 minutes | Serves 4

2 tablespoons soy sauce or tamari

3 heaping tablespoons fresh chives

2 tablespoons olive oil

3 tablespoons dry white wine

4 small-sized beef steaks

2 teaspoons smoked cayenne

pepper

½ teaspoon dried basil

½ teaspoon dried rosemary

1 teaspoon freshly ground black pepper

1 teaspoon sea salt, or more to taste

Firstly, coat the steaks with the cayenne pepper, black pepper, salt, basil, and rosemary.

Drizzle the steaks with olive oil, white wine, and soy sauce.

Finally, roast in the air fryer for 20 minutes at 172ºC. Serve garnished with fresh chives. Bon appétit!

Pork Bulgogi

Prep time: 30 minutes | Cook time: 15 minutes | Serves 4

1 onion, thinly sliced

2 tablespoons gochujang (Korean red chili paste)

1 tablespoon minced fresh ginger

1 tablespoon minced garlic

1 tablespoon soy sauce

1 tablespoon Shaoxing wine (rice cooking wine)

1 tablespoon toasted sesame oil

1 teaspoon sugar

¼ to 1 teaspoon cayenne pepper or gochugaru (Korean ground red pepper)

450 g boneless pork shoulder, cut into ½-inch-thick slices

1 tablespoon sesame seeds

60 ml sliced spring onionspring onions

In a large bowl, combine the onion, gochujang, ginger, garlic, soy sauce, wine, sesame oil, sugar, and cayenne. Add the pork and toss to coat. Marinate at room temperature for 30 minutes, or cover and refrigerate for up to 24 hours.

Arrange the pork and onion slices in the air fryer basket; discard the marinade. Set the air fryer to 204ºC for 15 minutes, turning the pork halfway through the cooking time.

Arrange the pork on a serving platter. Sprinkle with the sesame seeds and spring onionspring onions and serve.

Currywurst

Prep time: 15 minutes | Cook time: 12 minutes | Serves 4

235 ml tomato sauce

2 tablespoons cider vinegar

2 teaspoons curry powder

2 teaspoons sweet paprika

1 teaspoon sugar

¼ teaspoon cayenne pepper

1 small onion, diced

450 g bratwurst, sliced diagonally into 1-inch pieces

In a large bowl, combine the tomato sauce, vinegar, curry powder, paprika, sugar, and cayenne. Whisk until well combined. Stir in the onion and bratwurst.

Transfer the mixture to a baking pan. Place the pan in the air fryer basket. Set the air fryer to 204ºC for 12 minutes, or until the sausage is heated through and the sauce is bubbling.

Chapter 9 Desserts

Chapter 9 Desserts

Peanut Butter, Honey & Banana Toast

Prep time: 10 minutes | Cook time: 9 minutes | Serves 4

2 tablespoons unsalted butter, softened	2 bananas, peeled and thinly sliced
4 slices white bread	4 tablespoons honey
4 tablespoons peanut butter	1 teaspoon ground cinnamon

Spread butter on one side of each slice of bread, then peanut butter on the other side. Arrange the banana slices on top of the peanut butter sides of each slice (about 9 slices per toast). Drizzle honey on top of the banana and sprinkle with cinnamon.

Cut each slice in half lengthwise so that it will better fit into the air fryer basket. Arrange two pieces of bread, butter sides down, in the air fryer basket. Set the air fryer to 192°C cooking for 5 minutes. Then set the air fryer to 204°C and cook for an additional 4 minutes, or until the bananas have started to brown. Repeat with remaining slices. Serve hot.

Molten Chocolate Almond Cakes

Prep time: 5 minutes | Cook time: 13 minutes | Serves 3

Butter and flour for the ramekins	1 tablespoon plain flour
110 g bittersweet chocolate, chopped	3 tablespoons ground almonds
110 gunsalted butter	8 to 12 semisweet chocolate discs (or 4 chunks of chocolate)
2 eggs	Cocoa powder or icing sugar, for dusting
2 egg yolks	
50 g granulated sugar	Toasted almonds, coarsely chopped
½ teaspoon pure vanilla extract, or almond extract	

Butter and flour three (170 g) ramekins. (Butter the ramekins and then coat the butter with flour by shaking it around in the ramekin and dumping out any excess.)

Melt the chocolate and butter together, either in the microwave or in a double boiler. In a separate bowl, beat the eggs, egg yolks and sugar together until light and smooth. Add the vanilla extract. Whisk the chocolate mixture into the egg mixture. Stir in the flour and ground almonds.

Preheat the air fryer to 164°C.

Transfer the batter carefully to the buttered ramekins, filling halfway. Place two or three chocolate discs in the center of the batter and then fill the ramekins to ½-inch below the top with the remaining batter. Place the ramekins into the air fryer basket and air fry for 13 minutes. The sides of the cake should be set, but the centers should be slightly soft. Remove the ramekins from the air fryer and let the cakes sit for 5 minutes. (If you'd like the cake a little less molten, air fry for 14 minutes and let the cakes sit for 4 minutes.)

Run a butter knife around the edge of the ramekins and invert the cakes onto a plate. Lift the ramekin off the plate slowly and carefully so that the cake doesn't break. Dust with cocoa powder or icing sugar and serve with a scoop of ice cream and some coarsely chopped toasted almonds.

Mixed Berry Hand Pies

Prep time: 5 minutes | Cook time: 30 minutes | Serves 4

150 g granulated sugar	two equal portions
½ teaspoon ground cinnamon	1 teaspoon water
1 tablespoon cornflour	1 package refrigerated shortcrust pastry (or your own homemade pastry)
150 g blueberries	
150 g blackberries	
150 g raspberries, divided into	1 egg, beaten

Combine the sugar, cinnamon, and cornstarch in a small saucepan. Add the blueberries, blackberries, and ½ of the raspberries. Toss the berries gently to coat them evenly. Add the teaspoon of water to the saucepan and turn the stovetop on to medium-high heat, stirring occasionally. Once the berries break down, release their juice, and start to simmer (about 5 minutes), simmer for another couple of minutes and then transfer the mixture to a bowl, stir in the remaining ½ of the raspberries and let it cool.

Preheat the air fryer to 188°C.

Cut the pie dough into four 5-inch circles and four 6-inch circles.

Spread the 6-inch circles on a flat surface. Divide the berry filling between all four circles. Brush the perimeter of the dough circles with a little water. Place the 5-inch circles on top of the filling and press the perimeter of the dough circles together to seal. Roll the edges of the bottom circle up over the top circle to make a crust around the filling. Press a fork around the crust to make decorative indentations and to seal the crust shut. Brush the pies with egg wash and sprinkle a little sugar on top. Poke a small hole in the center of each pie with a paring knife to vent the dough.

Air fry two pies at a time. Brush or spray the air fryer basket with oil and place the pies into the basket. Air fry for 9 minutes. Turn the pies over and air fry for another 6 minutes. Serve warm or at room temperature.

Zucchini Bread

Prep time: 10 minutes | Cook time: 40 minutes | Serves 12

220 g coconut flour
2 teaspoons baking powder
150 g granulated sweetener
120 ml coconut oil, melted
1 teaspoon apple cider vinegar

1 teaspoon vanilla extract
3 eggs, beaten
1 courgette, grated
1 teaspoon ground cinnamon

In the mixing bowl, mix coconut flour with baking powder, sweetener, coconut oil, apple cider vinegar, vanilla extract, eggs, courgette, and ground cinnamon.

Transfer the mixture into the air fryer basket and flatten it in the shape of the bread.

Cook the bread at 176°C for 40 minutes.

Orange, Anise & Ginger Skillet Cookie

Prep time: 20 minutes | Cook time: 15 minutes | Serves 2 to 4

Cookie:
Vegetable oil
125 g plain flour, plus 2 tablespoons
1 tablespoon grated orange zest
1 teaspoon ground ginger
1 teaspoon aniseeds, crushed
¼ teaspoon kosher, or coarse sea salt

4 tablespoons unsalted butter, at room temperature
100 g granulated sugar, plus more for sprinkling
3 tablespoons black treacle
1 large egg
Icing:
60 g icing sugar
2 to 3 teaspoons milk

For the cookie: Generously grease a baking pan with vegetable oil. In a medium bowl, whisk together the flour, orange zest, ginger, aniseeds, and salt.

In a medium bowl using a hand mixer, beat the butter and sugar on medium-high speed until well combined, about 2 minutes. Add the treacle and egg and beat until light in color, about 2 minutes. Add the flour mixture and mix on low until just combined. Use a rubber spatula to scrape the dough into the prepared pan, spreading it to the edges and smoothing the top. Sprinkle with sugar.

Place the pan in the basket. Set the air fryer to 164°C and bake for 15 minutes, or until sides are browned but the center is still quite soft.

Let cool in the pan on a wire rack for 15 minutes. Turn the cookie out of the pan onto the rack.

For the icing: Whisk together the sugar and 2 teaspoons of milk. Add 1 teaspoon milk if needed for the desired consistency. Spread, or drizzle onto the cookie.

Spiced Apple Cake

Prep time: 15 minutes | Cook time: 30 minutes | Serves 6

Vegetable oil
2 diced & peeled Gala apples
1 tablespoon fresh lemon juice
55 g unsalted butter, softened
65 g granulated sugar
2 large eggs
155 g plain flour
1½ teaspoons baking powder

1 tablespoon apple pie spice
½ teaspoon ground ginger
¼ teaspoon ground cardamom
¼ teaspoon ground nutmeg
½ teaspoon kosher, or coarse sea salt
60 ml whole milk
Icing sugar, for dusting

Grease a 0.7-liter Bundt, or tube pan with oil; set aside.

In a medium bowl, toss the apples with the lemon juice until well coated; set aside.

In a large bowl, combine the butter and sugar. Beat with an electric hand mixer on medium speed until the sugar has dissolved. Add the eggs and beat until fluffy. Add the flour, baking powder, apple pie spice, ginger, cardamom, nutmeg, salt, and milk. Mix until the batter is thick but pourable.

Pour the batter into the prepared pan. Top batter evenly with the apple mixture. Place the pan in the air fryer basket. Set the air fryer to 176°C and cook for 30 minutes, or until a toothpick inserted in the center of the cake comes out clean. Close the air fryer and let the cake rest for 10 minutes. Turn the cake out onto a wire rack and cool completely.

Right before serving, dust the cake with icing sugar.

Vanilla Pound Cake

Prep time: 10 minutes | Cook time: 25 minutes | Serves 6

110 g blanched finely ground almond flour
55 g salted butter, melted
100 g granulated sweetener
1 teaspoon vanilla extract

1 teaspoon baking powder
120 ml full-fat sour cream
30 g full-fat cream cheese, softened
2 large eggs

In a large bowl, mix almond flour, butter, and sweetener.

Add in vanilla, baking powder, sour cream, and cream cheese and mix until well combined. Add eggs and mix.

Pour batter into a round baking pan. Place pan into the air fryer basket.

Adjust the temperature to 148°C and bake for 25 minutes.

When the cake is done, a toothpick inserted in center will come out clean. The center should not feel wet. Allow it to cool completely, or the cake will crumble when moved.

Coconut-Custard Pie

Prep time: 10 minutes | Cook time: 20 to 23 minutes | Serves 4

240 ml milk

50 g granulated sugar, plus 2 tablespoons

30 g scone mix

1 teaspoon vanilla extract

2 eggs

2 tablespoons melted butter

Cooking spray

50 g desiccated, sweetened coconut

Place all ingredients except coconut in a medium bowl.

Using a hand mixer, beat on high speed for 3 minutes.

Let sit for 5 minutes.

Preheat the air fryer to 164°C.

Spray a baking pan with cooking spray and place pan in air fryer basket.

Pour filling into pan and sprinkle coconut over top.

Cook pie for 20 to 23 minutes or until center sets.

Coconut Mixed Berry Crisp

Prep time: 5 minutes | Cook time: 20 minutes | Serves 6

1 tablespoon butter, melted

340 g mixed berries

65 g granulated sweetener

1 teaspoon pure vanilla extract

½ teaspoon ground cinnamon

¼ teaspoon ground cloves

¼ teaspoon grated nutmeg

50 g coconut chips, for garnish

Preheat the air fryer to 164°C. Coat a baking pan with melted butter. Put the remaining ingredients except the coconut chips in the prepared baking pan.

Bake in the preheated air fryer for 20 minutes.

Serve garnished with the coconut chips.

Pears with Honey-Lemon Ricotta

Prep time: 10 minutes | Cook time: 8 minutes | Serves 4

2 large Bartlett pears

3 tablespoons butter, melted

3 tablespoons brown sugar

½ teaspoon ground ginger

¼ teaspoon ground cardamom

125 g full-fat ricotta cheese

1 tablespoon honey, plus additional for drizzling

1 teaspoon pure almond extract

1 teaspoon pure lemon extract

Peel each pear and cut in half, lengthwise. Use a melon baller to scoop out the core. Place the pear halves in a medium bowl, add the melted butter, and toss. Add the brown sugar, ginger, and cardamom; toss to coat.

Place the pear halves, cut side down, in the air fryer basket. Set the air fryer to 192°C cooking for 8 to 10 minutes, or until the pears are lightly browned and tender, but not mushy.

Meanwhile, in a medium bowl, combine the ricotta, honey, and almond and lemon extracts. Beat with an electric mixer on medium speed until the mixture is light and fluffy, about 1 minute.

To serve, divide the ricotta mixture among four small shallow bowls. Place a pear half, cut side up, on top of the cheese. Drizzle with additional honey and serve.

Baked Apples and Walnuts

Prep time: 6 minutes | Cook time: 20 minutes | Serves 4

4 small Granny Smith apples

50 g chopped walnuts

50 g light brown sugar

2 tablespoons butter, melted

1 teaspoon ground cinnamon

½ teaspoon ground nutmeg

120 ml water, or apple juice

Cut off the top third of the apples. Spoon out the core and some of the flesh and discard. Place the apples in a small air fryer baking pan.

Insert the crisper plate into the basket and the basket into the unit. Preheat to 176°C.

In a small bowl, stir together the walnuts, brown sugar, melted butter, cinnamon, and nutmeg. Spoon this mixture into the centers of the hollowed-out apples.

Once the unit is preheated, pour the water into the crisper plate. Place the baking pan into the basket.

Bake for 20 minutes.

When the cooking is complete, the apples should be bubbly and fork tender.

Hazelnut Butter Cookies

Prep time: 30 minutes | Cook time: 20 minutes | Serves 10

4 tablespoons liquid monk fruit, or agave syrup

65 g hazelnuts, ground

110 g unsalted butter, room temperature

190 g almond flour

110 g coconut flour

55 g granulated sweetener

2 teaspoons ground cinnamon

Firstly, cream liquid monk fruit with butter until the mixture becomes fluffy. Sift in both types of flour.

Now, stir in the hazelnuts. Now, knead the mixture to form a dough; place in the refrigerator for about 35 minutes.

To finish, shape the prepared dough into the bite-sized balls; arrange them on a baking dish; flatten the balls using the back of a spoon.

Mix granulated sweetener with ground cinnamon. Press your cookies in the cinnamon mixture until they are completely covered.

Bake the cookies for 20 minutes at 154°C.

Leave them to cool for about 10 minutes before transferring them to a wire rack. Bon appétit!

Baked Cheesecake

Prep time: 30 minutes | Cook time: 35 minutes | Serves 6

50 g almond flour
1½ tablespoons unsalted butter, melted
2 tablespoons granulated sweetener
225 g cream cheese, softened
25 g powdered sweetener

½ teaspoon vanilla paste
1 egg, at room temperature
Topping:
355 ml sour cream
3 tablespoons powdered sweetener
1 teaspoon vanilla extract

Thoroughly combine the almond flour, butter, and 2 tablespoons of granulated sweetener in a mixing bowl. Press the mixture into the bottom of lightly greased custard cups.

Then, mix the cream cheese, 25 g of powdered sweetener, vanilla, and egg using an electric mixer on low speed. Pour the batter into the pan, covering the crust.

Bake in the preheated air fryer at 164ºC for 35 minutes until edges are puffed and the surface is firm.

Mix the sour cream, 3 tablespoons of powdered sweetener, and vanilla for the topping; spread over the crust and allow it to cool to room temperature.

Transfer to your refrigerator for 6 to 8 hours. Serve well chilled.

Mixed Berries with Pecan Streusel Topping

Prep time: 5 minutes | Cook time: 17 minutes | Serves 3

75 g mixed berries
Cooking spray
Topping:
1 egg, beaten
3 tablespoons almonds, slivered
3 tablespoons chopped pecans

2 tablespoons chopped walnuts
3 tablespoons granulated sweetener
2 tablespoons cold salted butter, cut into pieces
½ teaspoon ground cinnamon

Preheat the air fryer to 172ºC. Lightly spray a baking dish with cooking spray.

Make the topping: In a medium bowl, stir together the beaten egg, nuts, sweetener, butter, and cinnamon until well blended.

Put the mixed berries in the bottom of the baking dish and spread the topping over the top.

Bake in the preheated air fryer for 17 minutes, or until the fruit is bubbly and topping is golden brown.

Allow to cool for 5 to 10 minutes before serving.

Pumpkin Pudding with Vanilla Wafers

Prep time: 10 minutes | Cook time: 12 to 17 minutes | Serves 4

250 g canned no-salt-added pumpkin purée (not pumpkin pie filling)
50 g packed brown sugar
3 tablespoons plain flour
1 egg, whisked
2 tablespoons milk

1 tablespoon unsalted butter, melted
1 teaspoon pure vanilla extract
4 low-fat vanilla, or plain wafers, crumbled
Nonstick cooking spray

Preheat the air fryer to 176ºC. Coat a baking pan with nonstick cooking spray. Set aside.

Mix the pumpkin purée, brown sugar, flour, whisked egg, milk, melted butter, and vanilla in a medium bowl and whisk to combine. Transfer the mixture to the baking pan.

Place the baking pan in the air fryer basket and bake for 12 to 17 minutes until set.

Remove the pudding from the basket to a wire rack to cool.

Divide the pudding into four bowls and serve with the vanilla wafers sprinkled on top.

Printed in Great Britain
by Amazon

13447185R00038